THE
SHERLOCK HOLMES
CROSSWORD PUZZLE
BOOK

THE SHERLOCK HOLMES CROSSWORD PUZZLE BOOK

Famous Adventures
Fascinating Features

by **RUTH LAKE TEPPER**

Introduction by ROBERT LESLIE HIRTLE, JR., J.D.
With original illustrations by SIDNEY PAGET

GRAMERCY BOOKS
New York • Avenel

This edition is published by Gramercy Books,
distributed by Random House Value Publishing, Inc.,
40 Engelhard Avenue,
Avenel, New Jersey 07001,
by arrangement with Clarkson N. Potter, Inc.

Book design by Katy Homans, including silhouette
of Sherlock Holmes.

Printed and bound in the United States of America

Random House
New York • Toronto • London • Sydney • Auckland

Library of Congress Cataloging in Publication Data
Tepper, Ruth Lake.
    The Sherlock Holmes crossword puzzle book.

    Reprint. Originally published: New York: C.N. Potter,
c1977.
    1. Crossword puzzles. 2. Doyle, Arthur Conan, Sir,
1859-1930—Characters—Sherlock Holmes. I. Title.
[GV1507.C7T45 1986] 793.73'2   85-28683
ISBN: 0-517-60670-4

8 7 6 5 4 3 2

Dear Reader,

Why are crossword puzzles and detective stories so popular the world over? They entertain, of course; they test our wits. But even more, they provide the satisfaction of solving problems neatly and completely—and how often does that happen in this world?

After many years of being a solver of puzzles and a reader of mysteries, I became a maker of crossword puzzles, and it occurred to me that I could combine the two. So quicker than you can say "Sherlock Holmes," I thought of my favorite detective.

Rereading Conan Doyle to select the stories, I was surprised to find that although I am an old Holmes buff, I did not remember the solution to many of the mysteries. The stories were intriguing all over again, and so were the many facets of Holmes and his world (some of which I write about in the short features that appear here between puzzles).

Here, then, is the book: each puzzle consists of a Sherlock Holmes adventure and a crossword puzzle. The story is told in abridged form and it includes the problem, the action, and the clues, but not the solution. The solution is hidden among the words of the crossword puzzle. When you have solved the puzzle, fill in the words in the spaces indicated and a telegraphic message reveals the solution.

There is an epilogue to each story, on the same page as its crossword puzzle answer, that tells how Sherlock Holmes arrived at his solution and what happened after he unlocked the mystery.

Happy solving!

Ruth Lake Tepper

Contents

Introduction by Robert Leslie Hirtle, Jr.   9

STORIES & PUZZLES   13

     I. *A Scandal in Bohemia*   14

     II. *The Red-Headed League*   18

       221B Baker Street   22

     III. *A Case of Identity*   26

     IV. *The Man with the Twisted Lip*   30

       Did You Know That . . .?   34

       And Did You Know That . . .?   37

     V. *The Adventure of the Speckled Band*   38

     VI. *The Adventure of the Engineer's Thumb*   42

       The Scotland Yarders   46

     VII. *The Adventure of the Noble Bachelor*   50

     VIII. *The Adventure of the Beryl Coronet*   54

     IX. *Silver Blaze*   60

     X. *The Stockbroker's Clerk*   66

     XI. *The Reigate Puzzle*   70

     XII. *The Crooked Man*   76

     XIII. *The Naval Treaty*   80

     XIV. *The Adventure of the Empty House*   87

       Sherlock in Disguise   92

     XV. *The Adventure of the Norwood Builder*   96

     XVI. *The Adventure of Black Peter*   100

     XVII. *The Adventure of the Six Napoleons*   106

     XVIII. *The Adventure of the Three Students*   110

     XIX. *The Adventure of the Golden Pince-Nez*   116

The Case of George Edalji   122

XX. *The Adventure of the Missing Three-Quarter*   124

XXI. *The Adventure of the Abbey Grange*   130

     Baker Street Irregulars' Crossword Puzzle   136

SOLUTIONS & EPILOGUES   139

Introduction

When Ruth Lake Tepper asked me to comment on Sherlock Holmes's extralegal activities from my vantage point as a trial lawyer, I was delighted. Not only have I been an admirer of Conan Doyle's prismatic private detective, whose work in some ways parallels that of a trial lawyer, but I have been struck by Doyle's giving Holmes a strong sense of justice, and at the same time, giving him a wide latitude in dispensing the law or in dispensing with the law. Moreover, I have been struck by the public's acceptance of Holmes in the roles of judge and jury, and, on occasion, lawbreaker—a kind of private-eye folk hero.

Most serious crimes, especially murder, do not usually have eyewitnesses, and in such cases the parallels between the work of a trial lawyer and that of a detective are very close: the trial lawyer must build his case on circumstantial evidence, and the detective must solve his case through clues. Both must have certain traits in common: the abilities to observe, select, and correctly interpret their circumstantial evidence or clues.

In "A Scandal in Bohemia" Holmes makes a series of revelations to which Dr. Watson exclaims, "When I hear you give your reasons . . . the thing always appears to me to be so ridiculously simple that I could easily do it myself, though at each successive instance of your reasoning I am baffled until you explain your process. And yet . . . my eyes are as good as yours."

"Quite so. . . . You see, but you do not observe. The distinction is clear" is Holmes's reply.

And in "The Reigate Puzzle" Holmes states, "It is of the highest importance in the art of detection to be able to recognize, out of a number of facts, which are incidental and which are vital." The strength of Holmes as a detective is his ability to build the circumstantial case through his reasoning powers, through interpreting correctly what he has observed. In discussing circumstantial evidence in "The Boscombe Valley Mystery," Holmes calls it "a very tricky thing. . . . It may seem to point very straight to one thing, but if you shift your own point of view a little, you may find it pointing in an equally uncompromising manner to something entirely different."

Celebrated trial lawyers often act as detectives, gathering and interpreting circumstantial evidence. The renowned English defense advocate Sir Marshall Hall was such a lawyer, and, in fiction, Perry Mason is detective as much as lawyer.

It is when Holmes bends, breaks, rises above, or steps outside the law that the paths of the trial lawyer and the great detective diverge. While all of Holmes's extralegal activities have a moral basis, in "Silver Blaze" he points out, "I follow my own methods and tell as much or as little as I choose. That is the advantage of being unofficial." In "The Adventure of the Abbey Grange," comparing himself with a Scotland Yard inspector, Holmes says, ". . . what I know is unofficial . . . I have the right to private judgment . . ." Let us see how Holmes uses these rights.

In his methods, Holmes does not hesitate to break the law if it will help him to solve a case. During the adventure of "A Scandal in Bohemia," Holmes asks Watson if he would mind breaking the law and running the risk of being arrested by helping him. Watson replies, "Not in a good cause." Holmes assures him, "Oh, the cause is excellent!" Watson obliges by throwing a smoke bomb through Irene Adler's window, creating the illusion that her house is on fire. In "The Adventure of the Norwood Builder," Dr. Watson, on Holmes's instructions, strikes the match which sets fire to straw in the builder's house to smoke him out of his hiding place. It is noted that Holmes is an accessory before the fact to these fire incidents, using the diversionary tactics of Dr. Watson to cover his activities. Does the fact that Holmes solved the mysteries excuse his conduct entirely?

In at least six cases, Holmes is guilty of breaking and entering and/or burglary. In all of these cases, "the cause is excellent." Consider: to save a life, to fathom the mysterious actions of a wife, to solve a double murder, to stop a blackmailer's activities, to catch a spy, to prevent a young girl's marriage to a villain. It is interesting to note that in three of the cases, the police knew of Holmes's activities, but, as Watson remarks at the end of one of the stories, even "the rigid British law" can be stretched under certain circumstances. Holmes was not prosecuted.

At common law there was crime known as misprision of felony. This was the crime of failing to report the commission of a felony to the authorities. Today, prosecution for this crime has fallen into disuse, and unless some overt act is committed to make one an accessory there is no prosecution. Holmes, for reasons he considered ethical, sometimes concealed other people's crimes from the authorities. And in cases where a person of illustrious background turned to Holmes rather than to the police because he or she wanted to avoid a public scandal, Holmes's discretion could be counted on—again, based on ethical considerations. Doubtless, in the early days of their association, the jealous officers of Scotland Yard would have had Holmes prosecuted for misprision of felony had they had the chance.

Holmes felt that he had justifiable reasons for letting the criminals go free in three cases of thievery that he investigated: one, to avoid a public scandal after the stolen papers were recovered; another, because restitution was made in the form of money; and the third, because the stolen jewel was found, and because it was Christmas, and—but let Holmes tell it:

"After all, Watson . . . I am not retained by the police to supply their deficiencies. If Horner were in danger it would be another thing; but this fellow will not appear against him, and the case must collapse. I suppose that I am commuting a felony, but it is just possible that I am saving a soul. This fellow will not go wrong again; he is too terribly frightened. . . . Besides, it is the season of forgiveness."

When one considers Holmes's actions as judge and jury, it is not difficult to guess what Lestrade's reaction would have been could he have witnessed the following scene at any time— during the early, middle, or later days of their association. It takes place in "The Adventure of the Abbey Grange." Captain Jack Croker has killed Sir Eustace Brackenstall in self-defense—he claims. Holmes accepts his claim, based on the evidence he has gathered in the case.

". . . Well, it is a great responsibility that I take upon myself, but I have given [Inspector] Hopkins an excellent hint, and if he can't avail himself of it I can do no more. See here, Captain Croker, we'll do this in due form of law. You are the prisoner. Watson, you are a British jury. . . . I am the judge. Now, gentleman of the jury, you have heard the evidence. Do you find the prisoner guilty or not guilty?"

"Not guilty, my lord," says Watson.

"*Vox populi, vox Dei.* You are acquitted, Captain Croker. So long as the law does not find some other victim you are safe."

Among the more than twenty murder cases in which Holmes was involved, he allows four other killers to go free, based on his sense of justice and his right to private judgment. In "The Boscombe Valley Mystery," the murderer is an old man.

". . . You are yourself aware that you will soon have to answer for your deed at a higher court than the Assizes. I will keep your confession, and if McCarthy is condemned I shall be forced to use it. If not, it shall never be seen by mortal eye; and your secret, whether you be alive or dead, shall be safe with us."

In cases of murder or other crimes, where Holmes felt the crime was justified and did not violate his code of ethics, he did not betray the perpetrator, but neither did he stand in the way of Scotland Yard's inspectors—he usually counted on their reaching a dead end.

Holmes does not doubt the rightness of his decisions. In "The Final Problem," he remarks to Watson, "If my record were closed tonight I could still survey it with equanimity. . . . In over a thousand cases I am not aware that I have ever used my powers upon the wrong side . . ."

Conan Doyle presents Holmes as a man fiercely dedicated to eradicating evil wherever he finds it, but if a crime has extenuating circumstances, he permits Holmes to temper justice with mercy. The reader accepts this kind of poetic justice, probably because Holmes is depicted throughout the stories as a man of the highest principles, having no base or pecuniary motives, and with superior intelligence—capable of making right judgments.

In Mrs. Tepper's entertaining book, another kind of judgment is asked of the reader: to observe what Holmes has observed, to select the proper clues, and to interpret them. After comparing the solution with Holmes's, the reader can evaluate his or her own ability as a detective.

ROBERT LESLIE HIRTLE, JR., J. D.

Stories & Puzzles

A Scandal in Bohemia

To Sherlock Holmes she is always *the* woman. It was not that he felt any emotion akin to love for Irene Adler; all emotions were abhorrent to his cold, precise mind. And yet there was but one woman to him, the beautiful and audacious Irene.

Since Dr. Watson's recent marriage he had not seen Holmes for some time, so passing by Baker Street one night in March, '88, he looked in on his good friend. He found the tall, thin detective on the brink of a new case. Holmes handed him a mysterious, unsigned note that he had received in the last post.

There will call upon you tonight, at eight, a masked gentleman who desires to consult you on a matter of the deepest moment. Your services to the royal houses of Europe prove that you are one who may be trusted.

As Watson read the note there was an authoritative tap at the door, and a sumptuously dressed, masked man of Herculean stature entered. Holmes quickly unmasked the identity of the caller—the handsome Ormstein, King of Bohemia.

"I bind you both to secrecy for two years," cried the King. "I was mad—irresponsible! Five years ago, when I was Crown Prince, I met the adventuress Irene Adler—"

Holmes consulted his voluminous index, and read from it. "Prima donna, La Scala, thirty years old, living in London."

"She threatens to ruin me with a photograph of herself and me! She will not sell it, and foils all attempts to steal it. I would give half my kingdom for that photograph! I am to marry the daughter of the King of Scandinavia; Irene is furious. She swears to send it to the King—a very strict man—when my betrothal is made public. In three days!"

"You shall have it," promised Holmes, "before then."

Early next afternoon Watson, returning to Baker Street at Holmes's request, found him disguised as a stableman.

"You'll never guess what happened," said Holmes, laughing. "Posing as a groom, I went to the stables near Briony Lodge, Miss Adler's home. I learned that she drives out at five each day and returns at seven. She has one male visitor, a dashing lawyer, Godfrey Norton. As I was surveying Briony Lodge, Norton drove up, rushed in, ran out, shouting to the cabman to drive him to Regent Street, then to the Church of St. Monica. Minutes later Miss Adler darted into a cab, calling out, 'St. Monica!' Into a cab I went, racing after. I hurried into the church; it was empty save for the two and a clergyman. Suddenly Norton came towards me crying, 'You'll do!' and dragged me to the altar. And there I was, best man at the marriage!"

"A very unexpected turn of affairs," said Watson.

"I found my plans menaced—they might leave London immediately. But as they separated, Norton to return to the Temple, I heard her say, 'I shall drive out at five as usual.' Watson, I shall want your cooperation, if you don't mind breaking the law in a good cause. When Madame Irene returns at seven, we must be at Briony Lodge. I have arranged what is to occur. I will be conveyed into the house. The sitting room window will open; I will be visible to you. When I raise my hand, throw this smoke-rocket into the room and cry, 'Fire!' Then walk to the end of the street; I will rejoin you shortly."

The friends arrived at Briony Lodge at dusk. Holmes was disguised as a clergyman. An unusual number of people were strolling the quiet street. As Irene stepped out of her landau at seven, a fierce quarrel broke out around her. The clergyman dashed into the crowd to protect her, but reaching her he fell to the ground; a few droplets of red paint trickled down his face.

"He can't lie here," cried an onlooker. "May we bring him in, marm?" Irene graciously consented. Soon, through the open window, Watson could see her kindness as she attended to Holmes. Feeling rather ashamed, he threw the rocket into the room, filling it with smoke. In the ensuing confusion, Watson heard Holmes assuring everyone that it was a false alarm.

"You did nicely, Doctor," said Holmes, still in disguise, as they walked back to Baker Street. "I know where the photograph is; I knew she would show me. When a woman thinks that her house is on fire, she rushes to the thing she values most. It's in a recess behind a sliding panel. She half-drew it out, and replaced it when I cried false alarm."

"And now?" asked Watson.

"Tomorrow morning at eight we shall call on the lady, with the King. She will not be up; we will be shown into the sitting room. When she comes, we and the photograph will be gone."

They had reached Holmes's door, and as he searched for his key, a young man passing by called out, "Good-night, Mr. Holmes."

"Who the deuce was that?" asked Holmes, peering into the dark.

The King called at Baker Street next morning in a state of great excitement; the quest was almost ended. He was astonished to learn of Irene's marriage. Arriving at Briony Lodge, Holmes and his companions found an elderly woman waiting at the door.

"My mistress left this morning with her husband by the 5:15 train for the Continent, never to return."

"What!" Holmes, shocked, staggered back, white with chagrin. He pushed his way into the sitting room, tore back the sliding panel, pulled out a photograph—of Irene alone!—and a letter marked: "Sherlock Holmes, Esq. To be left till called for."

In this rare instance, Holmes was foiled—by a beautiful woman. How did Irene outwit him?

Across

1 Gelatin mold
6 Small wild horse
13 "Here's a pretty ___ of fish!"
15 Willa Cather's *My* ___
16 ___ down (told off)
17 Approaching
18 Monk's title
19 Seed covering
21 Stringed instruments
22 Else: Scot.
24 Rink attendants
26 Newspaper part
28 Naldi of the silent screen
32 Be affected
35 Ensued
37 A friend ___ (influential person)

40 Igneous rock
41 Justices of the Peace, at times
43 Desert gardens
44 "Passions spin the ___ . . ."
45 Perceiving
48 Keep in mind
49 Hibernia
53 Swiss house
57 Dark bluish-red
59 Spanish gold
60 Capital of Tasmania and man's name
62 Picked up the tab
64 Kind of green
65 "To every thing there is a ___ . . ."
66 Cat, panther, tiger, etc.
67 Entangle

Down

1 City in Ohio
2 ___ likely (admits of)
3 Liquid measures: Abbr.
4 "___ mad world."
5 Minister
6 "What a piece of work is a ___!"
7 Not equitably
8 Dishonor
9 Matador's adversary
10 Indigo
11 Columbus's ship
12 Cracks a joke
14 Decree
16 Presidential initials
20 Son of Eric the Red
23 Accompany
25 Pasture sounds
27 Small case
28 State of being a minor
29 Certainly, old style
30 Mal de ___

31 Summer drinks
32 Gangplank
33 And others: L. abbr.
34 Comb. form meaning "highest"
36 Ponce de ___
38 Establish a new residence
39 Waste allowance
42 ___ out of it (recover quickly)
46 Fills up with sediment
47 Hardens
48 Showed an old movie
50 Revolving part of a motor
51 Greek goddess of peace
52 Drowse
53 Maestro of the kitchen
54 "All the way, ___."
55 Cain's victim
56 Suborder of marine birds
58 Intend
61 Postal abbreviations
63 "Fair ___ star . . ."

Puzzle I: *A Scandal in Bohemia*

Solution and epilogue on page 140

— — — — — — — — — —, — — — — —

45 Across   44 Across   51 Down

— — — — — — — — — — — — —,

16 Across   63 Down   6 Down

— — — — — — — — — — — — — —.

35 Across   5 Down   54 Down

The Red-Headed League

Stopping by, one autumn day of '90, to see his friend, Sherlock Holmes, Dr. Watson found him in deep conversation with a stout, florid-faced, elderly gentleman with fiery red hair, a Mr. Jabez Wilson. The doctor was invited to listen to the singular narrative the perspiring visitor was relating.

"Here it is. This is what began it all," said Wilson, handing Watson an advertisement torn from a newspaper dated two months earlier. "Just read it for yourself!"

> To the Red-Headed League:
> On account of the bequest of the late Ezekiah Hopkins, there is now another vacancy open which entitles a member to a salary of £4 a week for nominal services. All red-headed men are eligible. Apply in person to D. Ross, League office, 7 Pope's Court, Fleet Street.

"My assistant, Vincent Spaulding, brought it to my attention," said Wilson. "He was surprised that I had never heard of the League, but I'm a stay-at-home fellow; I have a small pawnbroker's business in my home at Coburg Square. The League was founded by an American millionaire who was himself red-headed; he had great sympathy for red-headed men, so when he died he provided easy berths for them. Well, my trade had fallen off of late—I used to have two assistants, now I have only one, but Vincent is a smart fellow, willing to work for half wages to learn the business—"

"Most fortunate for you," observed Holmes.

"Oh, he has his faults, too," Wilson hastened to complain. "Never was such a one for photography. Snapping away with a camera, and diving down into the cellar to develop his pictures. But there's no vice in him. As I was saying, I decided to apply for the vacancy, and I never hope to see such a sight again! Fleet Street was choked with red-headed men of every shade, but not many had the real vivid flame-color like mine. There was a double line on the stair; I inched my way to the office."

The obese pawnbroker paused to mop his brow, then went on.

"The office had but two chairs and a table, behind which sat Mr. Ross, a small man with a head even redder than mine. I introduced myself; he exclaimed at my hair, pulled it hard to make sure it wasn't a wig, and then declared, 'The vacancy is yours!' Mr. Holmes, it was an ideal situation; the hours were from 10 A.M. to 2 P.M.; I was to copy out the Encyclopedia in Mr. Ross's office. The only condition made was that I be in the office the whole time, every day, or I would lose my billet; no excuse would avail. Oh, I kept my part of the bargain, all right, for eight weeks, and then this morning I found the door locked and a note saying, 'The Red-Headed League is Dissolved.' The landlord knew no Mr. Ross; he said that a solicitor, William Morris, had temporarily occupied the premises. I found that Mr. Morris had left a false address, so I came right away to you."

"And you did very wisely," said Holmes. "Graver issues may be involved in your case, though I understand your concern about your loss of income. What's he like, this Vincent Spaulding?"

"Small, quick in his ways, a splash of acid on his forehead."

"Are his ears pierced for earrings?" asked Holmes excitedly.

"Yes, sir. He told me a gypsy had done it for him."

"Ah, I thought as much!" cried Holmes. "Today is Saturday; I hope that by Monday we shall conclude this matter!"

After Wilson had gone, Watson shook his head, bewildered.

"Life," said Holmes reflectively, "is always far more daring than any effort of the imagination." Then, jumping up, he continued briskly, "But Sarasate plays at St. James's Hall this afternoon; let's take a look at Coburg Square on the way."

Three gilt balls and a sign reading "Jabez Wilson," on a corner house, announced the pawnbroker's place of business. Holmes knocked at the door; it was opened by Vincent Spaulding.

"I wished to ask how to go from here to the Strand."

"Third right, fourth left," replied the assistant promptly.

"Smart fellow," remarked Holmes as he and Watson walked away. "He is, in my judgment, the fourth smartest man in London. I saw on the knees of his trousers what I had expected to see: wear and tear. Now let us explore what lies around the corner."

It was a busy main artery, abutting Coburg Square.

"Let's see," said Holmes. "It's my hobby to have an exact knowledge of London. There's Mortimer's, the tobacconist, the newspaper shop, the Coburg branch of the City Bank, the Vegetarian Restaurant, and McFarlane's carriage depot. Now for Sarasate!"

Leaving St. James's Hall, Holmes asked Watson to be at Baker Street at ten that night. "There may be some danger, so kindly bring your revolver." The puzzled doctor drove home wondering how Holmes could foresee events, as though in a crystal ball.

At Baker Street at ten, Watson found that Holmes had been joined by two men; one he recognized as Peter Jones of Scotland Yard, and the other was a Mr. Merryweather, identified by Holmes as "our companion in tonight's adventure."

"It's the first Saturday night in years that I haven't had my game of whist," grumbled Mr. Merryweather.

"You will find," said Holmes, "that you will play for higher stakes tonight than you have ever done. For you, Mr. Merryweather, the stake will be £30,000 in gold, and for you, Jones, the man you have long wished to lay your hands on. Shall we go?"

Where were Holmes and his companions going? And what had been the purpose of the Red-Headed League?

Across

1 "Kiss me, _____ . . ."
5 Salad ingredient
9 _____ away the time
14 Female sheep
15 Hot place
16 Jots
17 Theatrical role
18 Prickly seedcase
19 Loam
20 Novice
21 Arm bone
22 _____ on thin ice
23 Actress Bayes
25 Malayan boat
27 Founding
30 Horse-drawn carriage
34 Feminine names
35 Astound
36 Kind of bet
37 Affirmative vote
38 Beginning

39 Sesame
40 Kind of spot
42 Caen's river
43 Get out of
45 Burrowed
47 Leader: Ger.
48 "Piping songs of pleasant _____ . . ."
49 He founded the Quaker State
50 Speech: Sp.
53 Scarlett's home
55 Great gull
59 "There is many _____ 'twixt the cup . . ."
60 Projecting rock
61 Singer Fitzgerald
62 Glacier angle
63 Japanese aborigine
64 Inert gas
65 "_____ shores of Tripoli."
66 Garden tool
67 Tick_____

Down

1 _____ on (continued)
2 Do _____ with (get rid of)
3 Veranda: Abbr.
4 Baltic nation
5 Bavarian city
6 Soft-palate appendage
7 American operetta composer
8 Fill with delight
9 28th U.S. president
10 Water-cooled tobacco pipes
11 Shrub genus
12 "To the _____ syllable of recorded time . . ."
13 Being: L.
24 Cricket field sides
26 Talk wildly
27 "Every _____ of the forest . . . "
28 "Here's looking _____!"
29 Strict

30 Witness _____
31 _____ the elbows (shabby)
32 Family of lions
33 Fisherman
35 Trolley
38 One and only
41 _____ Channel
43 Poetic contraction
44 Van Gogh
46 Pass, as time
47 "Half a _____ onward . . ."
49 Practical joke
50 Have, old style
51 Concerning
52 Stain
54 "Sempre Libera," for example
56 Bread spread
57 Political group
58 _____ holiday

Puzzle II: *The Red-Headed League*

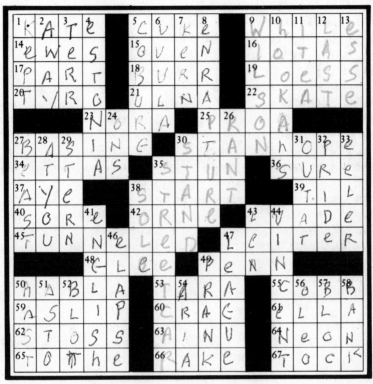

Solution and epilogue on page 141

To The COBURG BANK		
65 Across	5 Down	58 Down
"LEAGUE" KEPT WILSON		
47 Down	1 Down	9 Down
AWAY WhILe VINCENT		
2 Down	9 Across	44 Down
TUNNeLeD TO The BANK		
45 Across	65 Across	58 Down

221B Baker Street

*P*When Conan Doyle jotted down the address of 221B Upper Baker Street for his consulting detective (soon dropping the "Upper"), he could not have dreamed that the address was to become more widely known than the Prime Minister's. Yet its fame spread to the remote corners of the world, for it was at 221B Baker Street that most of the wonderful adventures of Sherlock Holmes and Dr. Watson began and ended.

To Baker Street came many of the varied cast of characters that crowd the stories, seeking the great man's help—kings and commoners, rich and poor, and the confused constabulary of Scotland Yard. To Baker Street came Lord St. Simon whose bride had vanished from the wedding breakfast; and a bevy of Violets and Marys in distress (Watson was to marry the dainty Mary Morstan); and the Prime Minister himself to tell of the dangerous loss of an inflammatory secret letter from a foreign leader.

It was ironic that Holmes, by temperament almost solitary, should have kept an open door. ("I was never a very sociable fellow, Watson," he had confided to his only friend.) But Holmes's work was his life. In the cause of his crusade against crime, the unsocial detective became cordial host to all the troubled visitors, and even villains, who knocked at the door.

The house on Baker Street was situated in a busy part of London, and in the sitting room of the modest, first-floor flat one could stand in the bow window and look down at the brisk traffic below, the passersby on the pavement, and the horses and carriages rattling along, or on foggy days see the thick, yellow London mist as it swirled about, blurring the row of houses across the street.

Inside the cluttered sitting room there was an atmosphere of informality that at once put callers at their ease: a crackling fire, a comfortable sofa, and Holmes himself, wearing his blue or purple dressing gown, likely to call out, "Good afternoon, Lestrade! You will find an extra tumbler upon the sideboard, and there are cigars in the box."

The gaslit suite, which had brought together the young, badly off Holmes and Watson—because neither could afford a decent place of his own— consisted of two bedrooms, bath, and the large sitting room and was reached by a flight of seventeen steps leading up from the downstairs hall. (Holmes, of course, knew the exact number of steps, but it had escaped Watson, no more observant than the rest of us.) The sitting room also served as dining room, office, laboratory, and library. Watson's bedroom on the second floor provided privacy. Motherly Mrs. Hudson, the landlady, was one of the wonders of the world. Altogether, a most satisfactory arrangement.

But there was a fly in the ointment, at least for Watson. How, he wondered, could Holmes, so methodical of thought, so neat of dress, be "in his personal habits one of the most untidy men that ever drove a fellow-lodger to

Holmes and Watson in front of the fire.

Holmes, in dressing gown, at the "chemical corner," with Watson.

distraction." The sitting room was filled with Victorian furniture, the bookshelves were crammed with Holmes's reference books, but it was the celebrated clutter of objects and papers strewn about the room, all the paraphernalia spelling home to Holmes, that unhinged Watson.

In the "chemical corner" stood an acid-stained table with a formidable array of bottles, test tubes, and retorts, at which Holmes would spend hours in abstruse research, his thin back bent over the boiling vessels, filling the room with horrible odors that sent Watson reeling out of the house.

There were cigars in the coal scuttle, tobacco in the toe of a Persian slipper, Holmes's violin case in one nook and the gasogene in another, scrapbooks and crumpled newspapers everywhere, and Watson's "great crux," stacks of Holmes's manuscripts and documents connected with his past cases, accumulating in every corner, waiting for Holmes to docket them and put them away.

The wall decorations had a patriotic flavor: on one wall a fine picture of General Gordon; on another, the initials of Victoria *Regina* sprayed in bullet pocks by the loyal Holmes. Watson took a dim view of Holmes's earsplitting indoor pistol practice.

But though he sometimes grumbled, on the whole, Watson cheerfully accepted these domestic drawbacks, overlooked in the exhilaration of joining Sherlock Holmes in his investigations: "Come, Watson, come! . . . . The game is afoot."

On quiet evenings the two friends would sit in their favorite armchairs on either side of the fire, Holmes puffing on his clay pipe, sending up clouds of blue smoke, philosophical or reminiscent, his Boswell taking it all in. Holmes was very attached to 221B Baker Street; he lived there almost a quarter of a century (until he retired to the country), although as his fame grew he could afford grander quarters.

Next time you are in London, don't plan to visit 221B Baker Street. It does not exist now, nor did it ever, except in our enthralled imaginations.

A Case of Identity

"This is one of my clients, or I am much mistaken," said Sherlock Holmes to Dr. Watson, as the two stood gazing down at Baker Street from Holmes's window. On the pavement opposite, a large young woman, with a boa around her neck and curling feather in her hat, paced nervously, glancing across at Holmes's residence.

"Oscillation on the pavement," continued Holmes, "always means an *affaire de coeur*. This maiden is not so much angry as perplexed, or grieved. But here she comes to resolve our doubts."

And in a moment the page boy announced Miss Mary Sutherland.

"Oh, Mr. Holmes," began the agitated lady, "I have heard from Mrs. Etherege that you found her husband when the police and everyone had given him up for dead. I'm not rich, but I have a hundred a year in my own right, besides the little I make as a typist, but I would give it all to know what has become of Mr. Hosmer Angel!" She brushed away a tear, and went on with her story. "My mother and Mr. Windibank—that is, my father—care nothing about his disappearance, won't go to the police—"

"Your father," said Holmes, "your stepfather, surely, since the name is different."

"Yes, my stepfather, but I call him father, though it sounds funny, for he is only five years older than myself. I wasn't pleased when my mother married so soon after father's death a man nearly fifteen years younger than herself. And Mr. Windibank made her sell father's plumbing business, for he felt superior, being a traveller in wines. They got £4700 for it."

"Your own little income," asked Holmes, with an intensity that rather surprised Watson, "does it come out of these funds?"

"Oh, no, sir. My uncle Ned left me New Zealand stock in the amount of £2500. But I can only touch the interest. As long as I live at home I don't wish to be a burden to them, so Mr. Windibank draws my interest every quarter and pays it over to mother, and I find I can do with what I earn at typewriting."

"You've made your position clear," said Holmes. "You may speak freely before Dr. Watson. Tell us about Mr. Hosmer Angel."

A flush stole over Miss Sutherland's face. "I met him at the gasfitters' ball," she said. "They sent tickets in father's memory. Mr. Windibank did not wish mother and me to go. He never did wish us to go anywhere! But he went off to France on business, so we went to the ball. After that, I met Mr. Angel twice for walks, but then father came back, and Mr. Angel couldn't come to our house because Mr. Windibank didn't allow visitors."

"Did Mr. Angel make no attempt to see you?" asked Holmes.

"He used to write every day. I took the letters in in the morning so there was no need for father to know. We were engaged after our first walk. Hosmer was a cashier in an office—"

26

"What office?"

"That's the worst of it, Mr. Holmes, I don't know. Also, he slept on the premises. I addressed my letters to him to the Leadenhall Street Post Office. He said that if they were sent to his office the other clerks would chaff him about having letters from a lady, so I offered to typewrite them, even the signature, like he did his, but he wanted them in my own handwriting. That shows you how fond he was of me."

"Can you tell me any other little things about Mr. Angel?"

"He was shy. He would rather walk with me in the evening than in the daylight, for he hated to be conspicuous. Very gentlemanly he was. Even his voice was gentle. He'd had the quinsy, and it left him with a whispering fashion of speech. He had black side-whiskers and moustache, and he wore tinted glasses because his eyes were weak, just as mine are."

"Well, what happened when Mr. Windibank went to France again?"

"Hosmer came to our house and proposed that we should marry before father came back. He was in dreadful earnest and made me swear on the Testament that whatever happened I would always be true to him. We arranged to be married at St. Savior's on Friday. Hosmer came for mother and me in a hansom, but as there were two of us he put us both into it and he took another cab. We got to the church first, and when his cab drove up we waited for him to step out, but he never did! The cabman said that he could not imagine what had become of him, for he had seen him get in with his own eyes."

"You have been very shamefully treated," said Holmes, as Mary began to sob. "How did your mother take the matter?"

"She was angry, and said I was never to speak of Hosmer."

"And your father? Did you tell him when he returned?"

"Yes, and he seemed to think, with me, that something had happened to Hosmer, and that I should hear of him again. As he said, if Hosmer had borrowed my money, or if he had married me and got my money, that might be a reason for his disappearance, but Hosmer never took a shilling of mine. Oh, what shall I do?"

"I shall look into the case for you, " said Holmes. "Above all, let Mr. Angel vanish from your thoughts as he has from your life. I fear you will not see him again. Please leave me any letters of his which you can spare, and your address and your father's place of business. Let the whole incident be a sealed book, and do not allow it to affect your life."

"You are very kind, Mr. Holmes, but I shall be true to Hosmer."

When she had gone, Holmes remarked to Watson, "I shall write to Windibank to arrange an appointment to discuss this lamentable problem with him. I know the answer, but Miss Mary wouldn't believe me; only time will part her from her delusion."

From Mary's story alone, Holmes deduced the plot behind her suitor's courtship and disappearance. Were you able to match him?

Across

1 "____ a joyful noise . . ."
5 Lucre
9 Member of B.P.O.E.
12 Feminine name
13 Courtyard
14 "Once ____ a midnight dreary . . ."
15 Hamlet's hated relative
17 Roman tyrant
18 Rescuer
19 Decline
20 "Zing! ____ the strings . . ."
21 Of a region
23 Mine yield
25 Lacking
28 Weddings
32 Dies ____
33 "But I have promises ____ . . ."
35 Teachers' org.
36 Heroine of *I Pagliacci*
38 Jurisdiction: Comb. form
39 Indications
41 Parisian summer
42 ____ a doornail
45 New York baseball team
46 Clerical lectures
48 Baseball error, for example
50 Hardwood tree
51 Blood condition: Suffix
52 Asterisk
55 Exclamations of surprise
57 Kind of tax
61 Sacred
62 Bulletin issued to subscribers
64 Literary collections
65 Jalopy
66 Volcano in Sicily
67 Pronoun
68 Ages
69 Easy ____ it

Down

1 Kind of production
2 Canadian province: Abbr.
3 Capital of the Ukraine
4 Atoned for
5 Tap lightly
6 Singer Merman
7 Dear: Ger.
8 Refrained
9 Fencing sword
10 Forsaken, old style
11 Tie the ____
13 Father or mother
14 Single
16 "____ have seen God face to face . . ."
22 Greek marketplaces
24 Tears
25 Chianti and claret
26 Mountain crest
27 Consumer advocate
28 Suited
29 "Look homeward, ____ . . ."
30 ____ hand (helped)
31 Impudent
34 Glove leather
37 Fusses
40 Wedged in
43 Heighten
44 Figure of speech
47 "My ____ asleep by thy murmuring stream . . ."
49 ____ qua non
51 Egyptian dam
52 Ruler of Iran
53 Musical sound
54 Winged
56 Protagonist
58 Holy Roman emperor
59 Word on Belshazzar's wall
60 Epochs
63 Wall and Main: Abbr.

Puzzle III: *A Case of Identity*

Solution and epilogue on page 142

___ ___ ___ ___ ___ ___   ___ ___ ___ ___ ___   ___ ___ ___ ___ ___ ___ ,

25 Across   47 Down   57 Across

___ ___ ___ ___ ___ ___ ___ ___ ___   ___ ___ ___ ___ ___ ___

15 Across   28 Down

" ___ ___ ___ ___ ___ " ___ ___   ___ ___ ___ ___   ___ ___ ___   ___ ___ ___ ___ ___ .

29 Down   33 Across   67 Across   14 Down

The Man with the Twisted Lip

O ne night in June '89, an errand of mercy had brought Dr. Watson to an opium den in the east of the City; he was in search of a patient who was an addict. Having found him, he was guiding the man down a narrow passage when he felt a tug at his coattail, and a voice whispered, "Walk past me, then look back." The words came from a wrinkled man with an opium pipe dangling from his lips. Watson took two steps forward, and looked back. The old man was Sherlock Holmes!

"What on earth are you doing here?" Watson whispered.

"Send your friend home in a cab," said Holmes, "and wait for me outside. Send a note to your wife that you are joining me."

Watson found it difficult to refuse any of Holmes's requests, and soon he was in a carriage driving out of town with Holmes.

"That den," said Holmes, "is the vilest murder-trap on the whole riverside, and I fear Neville St. Clair has entered it never to leave it more. I had hoped in vain for a clue tonight. We are going to The Cedars, Mr. St. Clair's home near Lee, in Kent. I am staying there while I conduct the inquiry."

"But I am all in the dark," said Watson.

"I shall explain. It's good to have someone to talk to. What shall I say to his wife? The case seems simple, yet—"

"Please proceed," said Watson.

"In 1884 St. Clair, who appeared to have money, came to Lee, took a large villa, and married a young lady, by whom he now has two children. He had no occupation, but was interested in several companies, and went into town each morning, returning by the 5:15 at night. He is a handsome man of thirty-seven, a good husband and father, and he has no money troubles.

"Last Monday St. Clair went into town as usual, saying that he would bring his little boy home a box of blocks. His wife received a telegram the same day, to the effect that a packet was waiting for her at Aberdeen Shipping—which is located near the opium den. Mrs. St. Clair picked up the parcel, was on her way home at 4:30, when a very strange thing occurred.

"As she walked past the opium den, she suddenly heard a cry, and saw her husband looking down at her and, it seemed to her, beckoning to her from a second-floor window of the building. She distinctly saw his face; he was very agitated. He then vanished suddenly, as though forcefully plucked back.

"She tried to ascend the stairs, but was pushed into the street by the den's manager. By good luck, she ran into a police inspector who took her up the stairs. There was no sign of St. Clair. The second floor's only occupant is a scarred cripple. He and the manager swore that no one else had been in the front room, but Mrs. St. Clair, noticing a box on a table, tore the lid from it, and out cascaded the child's blocks!

"The back bedroom faces a wharf; between the wharf and the window is a narrow strip, dry at low tide; water fills it at high tide. There were traces of blood on the windowsill. Behind a curtain in the front room were all of St. Clair's clothes but his coat. Out the window he must have gone, and drowned.

"The manager, who had been at the foot of the stairs at the start, could be no more than an accessory, but the cripple, Hugh Boone, was certainly the last to see St. Clair alive. Boone is a well-known professional beggar, with a shock of red hair and a face disfigured by a horrible scar, who reaps a good harvest.

"The inspector was somewhat tardy in arresting him, but did so after he noticed bloodstains on his shirt sleeve. The rascal pointed to his finger, which was cut at the nail. He swore that St. Clair's clothes were a mystery to him. The clothes are indeed a mystery! Boone was removed to the police station. When the tide ebbed, St. Clair's coat was found in the mud. What do you think they found in the pockets?"

"I can't imagine."

"Pennies, hundreds of them! A working hypothesis is that after Boone thrust St. Clair through the window, it struck him that he must get rid of the telltale clothes, and he was in the act of weighting them and throwing them out when Mrs. St. Clair and the inspector came up. But Boone has no record against him; his life has been very quiet and innocent—and why kill St. Clair?"

They had reached the villa; a blonde woman stood in the doorway, eagerly awaiting Holmes. "Well?" she cried, but Holmes had no news for her. He introduced Watson, whom she welcomed warmly.

As they went inside, Mrs. St. Clair turned to Holmes. "Tell me frankly, Mr. Holmes, do you think Neville is alive?"

"Frankly, madam, I do not," said Holmes gravely.

"Then explain how I received this letter from him—today!"

"What!" roared Holmes, snatching the letter from her hand. "Are you sure this is your husband's handwriting?"

"He wrote it hurriedly, but I am sure."

The letter implored Mrs. St. Clair not to be frightened. "All will come well," it said. "There is an error. Wait in patience."

"Posted today," said Holmes, "but possibly written on Monday."

"Oh, don't discourage me! I *know* he's well! There's so keen a sympathy between us! On Monday he cut himself in the bedroom, and I in the dining room rushed upstairs though I hadn't heard a sound!"

Holmes was dubious; he again questioned Mrs. St. Clair about her husband's habits. She assured him that he had never shown any signs of taking opium. When they retired it was obvious to Watson that Holmes would spend the night thinking about the case.

"Wake up, Watson," cried Holmes in the morning. "I have it!"

Two clues helped Holmes solve the mystery. Can you guess the solution and identify the clues?

31

Across

1 The two
5 Bedouins
10 Bleat
13 Of the field: L.
14 Columbus's birthplace
15 "To thine own ____ be true . . ."
16 Raced
17 Boca ____
18 "Ay, ____ her tattered ensign down!"
19 Ice cream concoction
21 Enrolls
23 General Robert ____
25 British peer
26 Reinforcements for heavy boots
30 Legally obligated
34 Exclamation of triumph
35 ____ course (eventually)
37 Fathers
38 Hindu garment
40 Action: It.

42 Tatters
43 Antler tip
45 Home on the range
47 Neckline shape
48 Transmitter
50 Swimmers
52 Beaver State: Abbr.
54 ____ price on (evaluate)
55 Kind of tree
58 Menace
62 ____ and tear
63 Legislate
65 Unusual
66 No ifs, ____, or buts
67 Bandy words
68 Always
69 Eyelid inflammation
70 Midterms
71 College administrator

Down

1 Chaliapin, for example
2 Former Russian secret service org.
3 Train: Sp.
4 Concealed
5 Concurring
6 Ginger plant
7 Opposed
8 American frontiersman
9 Huarache
10 Root vegetable
11 Exclamation of sorrow
12 Second largest continent: Abbr.
15 Michigan lake
20 Russian mountain range
22 Author of *Trinity*
24 Mormon priest
26 Metal fasteners
27 Chicago airport
28 Munchausen's title
29 Black-eyed ____

31 Shout of approval
32 French painter
33 Letters
36 Heating lamps
39 Inside a building
41 Musical groups
44 Feminine nickname
46 "Thirty days ____ September . . ."
49 Warm over
51 ____ and feathered
53 Kind, as of art
55 Coin
56 Baroness's title
57 Droops
59 Roof edge
60 Tract
61 Sea swallow
62 "The queen ____ in the parlor . . ."
64 "This was the most unkind-
   est ____ of all."

Puzzle IV:
The Man with the Twisted Lip

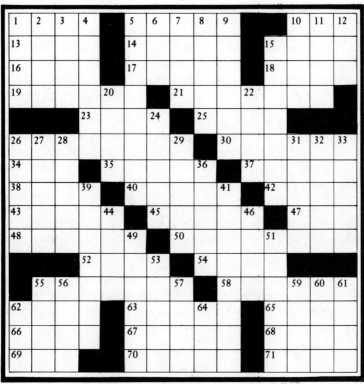

Solution and epilogue on page 143

—— —. —— —— —— —— —— —— —— —— —— —— :

15 Down   62 Down   8 Down

—— —— —— —— —— —— —— —— —— —— , —— —— —

4 Down   55 Across   1 Across

—— —— —— —— —— —— .

64 Down   15 Across

Did You Know That . . . ?

● If you are ever on a quiz show and are asked the names of the two most famous characters in all of English literature, you'll score if you answer, "Sherlock Holmes and Watson."

● Sherrinford Holmes was Conan Doyle's first choice of name for his great detective. He changed the name before the first Sherlock Holmes story was published. Sherlock was most likely named after the Sherlocks of Sherlockstown, the family whose grounds bordered on the ancestral Doyle estate in Ireland.

● Sherlock's last name was probably chosen in honor of Oliver Wendell Holmes, the American author of *The Autocrat of the Breakfast Table*—like Doyle, a writer and physician. To Doyle's great sorrow he was never able to meet the man he revered, as Holmes died shortly before Doyle made his first lecture tour of the United States.

● The most commonly quoted phrase in the Holmes lexicon, and the one supposedly most characteristic of him, does not appear anywhere in the more than thousand pages of the Holmes saga. There is a rare "Elementary," and Holmes often says, "my dear Watson," but he has never said, "Elementary, my dear Watson."

● While Sherlock was still Sherrinford, Watson was called Ormond Sacker. Doyle reconsidered this rather fancy name and gave the doctor the solid, dignified one of John H. Watson.

● Sherlock Holmes never wore a deerstalker. The renowned hunting cap with front and back visors, the symbol that immediately identifies Holmes all over the world, was the idea of Sidney Paget, the original illustrator of *The Adventures of Sherlock Holmes*. Sidney often wore a deerstalker on walks in the country; in an inspired moment he placed it on his brother Walter's head when he posed him as Sherlock.

● In 1886 Conan Doyle, in need of cash and to advance his writing career, sold the copyright of his first Holmes novel, *A Study in Scarlet*, for the now famous (or notorious) sum of £25.

● Doyle was so gifted a storyteller and so fluent a writer that he could work on his complicated stories under conditions that many writers would consider difficult. He did not mind if people came into the room where he was writing, or if they talked; he would even join in the conversation from time to time.

Holmes, wearing the deerstalker, expounds a theory to Watson.

Death struggle at the Reichenbach Falls.

And Did You Know That . . . ?

• Holmes's innovative procedures and theories were studied and adopted by police agencies in many parts of the world, from Europe to Asia to Africa. The Egyptian and the French police used his adventures as texts, and the Sûreté honored Doyle by naming its crime laboratories for him.

• As Holmes grew more and more real to his admiring public, Doyle's identity began to merge in the minds of his readers with that of his literary creation. His mail frequently contained pleas for help in solving real problems; being a man of broad sympathies, Doyle helped wherever he could. He was most successful in locating missing persons; in these cases he could often deduce the reason for the disappearance and the logical place to look for the vanished one, who might be a man beset with financial worries or a fiancé with cold feet.

• Like lesser mortals, that sinister genius of evil, Professor Moriarty, whose name with its hissing s's and rolling r's sends a thrill of terror through us, also had a first name. It was seldom used in the Holmes stories. His first name was James. By a slip of Doyle's pen, Colonel Moriarty, the Professor's devoted brother, was also named James.

• Although the faithful Watson is famous as Holmes's indefatigable Boswell, he did not narrate all the sixty stories that make up the Holmes epic. Sherlock Holmes himself related two of the later tales, and two are told in the third person.

• In 1889 an agent of *Lippincott's Magazine*, in England to commission books from British authors who had had some success in America, invited two writers (not acquainted with each other) to discuss the matter with him at dinner. It turned out to be a historic literary meal; as a result of it Conan Doyle wrote his second Sherlock Holmes novel, *The Sign of Four*, for Lippincott, and the other dinner guest, Oscar Wilde, wrote *The Picture of Dorian Gray*.

• The Reichenbach Falls in Switzerland, where Holmes almost lost his life in the death struggle with Moriarty, is one of the highest in the Alps. But now the torrential waters, so magnificently described by Doyle in "The Final Problem," have been tamed by the construction of a hydroelectric project.

The Adventure of the Speckled Band

Sherlock Holmes and Dr. Watson found a young woman, shivering with fear, waiting in their sitting room one April morning of '83. She was Helen Stoner, stepdaughter of Dr. Grimesby Roylott of Stoke Moran, and she told a story of dread and terror.

"I live with my stepfather, the last survivor of an old Saxon family. Once they were rich, now only a few acres and the mortgaged house remain. My widowed mother married Dr. Roylott in India; my sister, Julia, and I were children then. One day Dr. Roylott beat his native butler to death; when he had served his term we all returned to London. Soon after, my mother was killed in a railway accident. She had bequeathed all her money to Dr. Roylott while we lived with him, with the provision that he pay us a large annual sum if we married. Dr. Roylott abandoned his practice, and took us to live in the ancestral manor."

The young woman, who was dressed in black, sighed deeply.

"A terrible change came over our stepfather at that time. He shut himself in the house, and emerged only to brawl; the tropics had worsened his inherited bad temper. Now he has no friends but the gypsies, whom he allows to camp on his acres. He imports animals from India, and lets them roam freely; the cheetah and the baboon terrify the villagers.

"Oh, Mr. Holmes, my poor sister and I had no great joy in our lives. She died two years ago, within a fortnight of her wedding. It is of that terrible event that I wish to speak."

"Pray be precise as to details," said Holmes.

"Only one wing of the house is used. First of the adjoining bedrooms on the ground floor is Dr. Roylott's, next is Julia's, the corner one mine. There's no communication between them, but the doors open on the same corridor, the windows on the lawn.

" 'Helen,' said my sister that fatal night, 'have you ever heard anyone whistle in the dead of night, as I recently have?'

"I told her that I had not. I heard her lock her door after she had left my room; we always locked our doors because of the animals. I shall never forget Julia's wild scream in the night. As I ran into the hall I seemed to hear a low whistle, and then a clanging sound. I saw my sister's door unlock; she swayed in the doorway, then fell, writhing in pain. Dr. Roylott ran from his room to help her. Just before she died, she shrieked, 'It was the band! The speckled band!' Oh, it was horrible!

"The coroner could discover no cause of death, and declared that she was alone when she met her end—the door was locked, the windows blocked by iron bars which are secured every night, the walls and floor solid, the chimney barred by staples. In her hands were found a charred match and a matchbox. I believe she died of shock. Perhaps, Mr. Holmes, by 'speckled band' she meant the band of gypsies, who wear spotted headkerchiefs?"

"Perhaps," said Holmes. "But please go on."

"I became engaged to Percy Armitage last month. Two days ago repairs were started on the house; my bedroom wall has been pierced, so I have moved into Julia's room. Imagine my horror when I heard last night a low whistle. Oh, Mr. Holmes—"

"If I were to come to Stoke Moran today, would it be possible to see these rooms without your stepfather's knowledge?"

"Yes, he spoke of coming into town today on business."

"Then you may expect us early in the afternoon."

When Miss Stoner had gone, Holmes said to Watson, "The mystery may be cleared along these lines: whistles in the night, Dr. Roylott's gypsy band, his pecuniary motive for preventing Julia's marriage, a clanging window bar falling back into place."

"But what, then, did the gypsies do?" wondered Watson.

"I cannot imagine. That's why we're going to Stoke Moran."

Arriving there, Holmes inspected the building, observing that there seemed to be little need for repairs. He asked Miss Stoner to bar her bedroom window; standing outside, he found it impossible to raise the bars. Next, he examined Julia's room. Her bed was against the wall, clamped to the floor.

"That bell-rope hanging down the wall beside the bed looks newer than other things in the room. Did Julia ask for it?"

"No, it was put there two years ago, but she never used it."

"Why, it's a dummy," said Holmes, tugging the bell-rope. "It's fastened to a hook above the little ventilator opening."

"How absurd," said Miss Stoner. "I never noticed! The ventilator—it lets in Dr. Roylott's cigar smoke—was also put in then."

"Strange," muttered Holmes. "May we see Dr. Roylott's room?"

The room was plainly furnished, as were the others. Holmes examined it carefully; a large iron safe interested him.

"What's in here?" he asked. "Not a cat, is there?" He indicated a small saucer of milk on top of the safe.

"No, just papers, I think. The milk may be for the cheetah."

Another object caught Holmes's eye—a small dog lash, tied so as to make a loop of whipcord, hung on a corner of the doctor's bed. "What do you make of that, Watson? Interesting!"

Holmes's face was grim as he concluded his investigation.

"Follow my advice in every respect, Miss Stoner—your life may depend on it! My friend and I must spend the night in Julia's room. We are now going to the village inn; when Dr. Roylott retires, put a lamp in the window as a signal, then go to your own room—you can manage there for one night."

It was midnight when Holmes and Watson began their dangerous vigil in Julia's darkened room. Watson had brought a pistol, Holmes a cane and matches. They waited tensely, in silence.

Holmes had deduced the means Roylott used to kill Julia. Did you? What was it?

Across

1 In a violent rage
5 Stravinsky
9 Tiny particle
13 Involving no risk
14 Kind of dance
15 Cleave
16 Rapid pace
17 Retorted: Slang
19 Haberdasher
21 Persian tiger
22 Guido's high note
23 Rainbow
25 Thick slice
27 Nickname
30 Scribble
34 Old Indic language: Abbr.
35 Atomizer
37 Fraulein's name
38 ". . . a _____ is in the streets."
40 "_____ on her roses, roses . . ."

42 Slim
43 "_____ the best of times . . ."
45 Third son of Adam, et al.
47 Month: Abbr.
48 Discoverer of Mississippi River
50 Porcine
52 Sieve
54 Suffixes meaning "language of"
55 Exclamations of contempt
58 "One _____, one land, one heart . . ."
60 Called
64 Advantageous
67 About aircraft
68 Poetic name for Ireland
69 Power
70 "Oh, Wilderness were Paradise _____!"
71 Lasso
72 Noted Italian family
73 Diving bird

Down

1 Sholem _____, U.S. novelist
2 Jaw: L.
3 "That's the humor _____."
4 Held back
5 "The poet's eye, _____ fine frenzy rolling . . ."
6 Schools of whales
7 Approves: Slang
8 Revolts
9 Curved line
10 Tot
11 Ellipsoid
12 Prefix meaning "altered"
14 Pinches pennies
18 "Leave not _____ behind."
20 Greek god of love
24 Spanish muralist and family
26 Unruly child
27 Fly _____ (send up a trial balloon)
28 Sprouts
29 Nostrils
31 One of The Three Musketeers

32 What one?
33 Fasting period
34 Glided
36 ". . . and _____ fancy ourselves eternal."
39 Ancient temple
41 Kind of stop
44 Starched
46 Snicker_____ (large dagger)
49 "Variety's the very spice _____."
51 Haifa's country
53 Stuffed tortillas
55 Over: Ger.
56 Leander's beloved
57 Small piece
59 Surrounded
61 Minus: It.
62 Slangy suffix
63 Swallow
65 Compass point
66 Expert

Puzzle V:
The Adventure of the Speckled Band

1	2	3	4	■	5	6	7	8	■	9	10	11	12
13				■	14				■	15			
16				■	17				18				
19			20		■	21				■	22		

Solution and epilogue on page 144

_____ _____ _____ _____

14 Across 32 Down 34 Down 63 Down

_____ , _____ _____

71 Across 17 Across

_____. ___ ___ _____ __-

41 Down 43 Across 4 Down

____ .

13 Across

The Adventure of the Engineer's Thumb

Good heavens," cried Dr. Watson, "this is a terrible accident!" A young man, weary and pale-looking, had just shown the doctor his hand—with a red, spongy surface where his thumb used to be.

It was seven o'clock of a summer morning, not long after Watson's marriage; the young man, Victor Hatherley, a hydraulic engineer, had knocked at the doctor's door in great distress.

"No, not an accident," said Hatherley, "a murderous attack with a cleaver! I have to tell the police of last night's events, but they won't believe me."

"Then you must see my friend, Sherlock Holmes," said Watson.

When the wound had been dressed the two men set out for Baker Street, where Holmes lent a sympathetic ear to Hatherley's tale.

"I am an orphan and a bachelor," said the engineer, "residing alone. Two years ago I went into business for myself—with little success. That is why I accepted Colonel Lysander Stark's strange commission; he offered me fifty guineas for an hour's work. The thinnest man I have ever seen, he came to my office yesterday; though I knew nothing of him, he knew all about me. Before saying what he wanted, he swore me to absolute secrecy.

" 'I need your opinion about a hydraulic press that is losing some force. Show us what's wrong; we'll set it right. Come tonight by the midnight train to Eyford. I'll meet you with a carriage; our place is six miles from town.'

"The fee was tenfold what I should have asked, but I inquired if I might come at a more convenient hour. He would not agree.

" 'I discovered a deposit of fuller's earth in my land,' he said, 'a very valuable product. The deposit forms a link between two larger ones in my neighbors' grounds; they do not know about the clay. My friends and I do not have the money to buy their land, but we are secretly working our deposit to earn it. A hydraulic engineer must not be seen at our house!"

" 'But why do you use a press? Is not the clay dug up?'

" 'Ah, then we press it into bricks,' said he, 'so that we may remove them without revealing what they are made of.'

"His story didn't satisfy me, but I went to Eyford nevertheless. I was the only passenger alighting. Stark was waiting with a carriage; we sped away as fast as the horse would go."

"One horse?" interjected Holmes. "Tired-looking or fresh?"

"Only one, fresh and glossy. We drove for at least an hour; it must have been nearer twelve miles than six to his house. I could not see out the carriage's frosted windows, but the road was flat. Arriving, we stepped out of the carriage right into the hall. It was dark inside, but suddenly a young woman with a lamp appeared. Stark spoke gruffly to her, pushing her away.

"'Wait in here,' he said to me, and showed me into a small room. 'I'll be back in an instant.'

"I tried to look out the window; it was shuttered. Unexpectedly, the young woman with the lamp opened the door. She was fearful, and held up a shaking finger to warn me to be silent.

" 'Go, go,' she whispered, 'get away before it is too late!'

"But I am rather headstrong, and declared that I would stay. At the sound of footsteps, she vanished. Colonel Stark came in, accompanied by a stocky man who was introduced as Mr. Ferguson.

" 'We'll take you up to see the machine now,' said Stark.

"We went up a winding staircase, and stopped at a low door, which the colonel unlocked. He and I entered a small room.

" 'We are now actually inside the hydraulic press,' he said. 'The ceiling is really the piston end; it comes down with tons of force to this metal floor. It is worked from the outside.'

"I took the lamp, examined the outer water-columns, pointing out the trouble spot. Back inside, I noted that the walls were wood. I bent to look at a metallic deposit covering the floor.

" 'Is *this* fuller's earth?' I asked, annoyed that Stark thought I would believe the powerful press was used to make clay bricks.

" 'You shall soon know all about the machine!' he cried. He stepped outside, slammed the door, and turned the key. Suddenly I heard the clank of the levers; he had started the machine! I shall never forget the terror that swept over me! But as I crouched down, a panel in the wall opened, and I threw myself through. The panel closed; I heard the crash of the lamp inside.

" 'Come, come!' cried my savior, the young woman who had befriended me. 'They will be here in a moment!' I ran with her down a corridor, into a room. 'Jump, it's your only chance!'

"I did not want to leave her to Stark's mercy, so I clambered out the window to watch, clinging to the sill as Stark rushed in madly, cleaver in hand. She tried to stop him, but he cut at me wildly. I felt a dull pain, and dropped to the garden. I staggered, then fell unconscious. I awoke in the morning, lying by the roadside. I don't know why I wasn't killed."

"We shall go to Scotland Yard at once," said Holmes.

Three hours later, on a train bound for Eyford, were Holmes, Watson, Hatherley, Inspector Bradstreet, and a plain-clothes man. Bradstreet had drawn a circle on a map, with a radius of ten miles and Eyford for its center.

"Stark's place is somewhere near the circumference," he said, "but I wish I knew at just what point. I think it's south—more deserted there."

Hatherley thought it was east, the plain-clothes man west (small villages there), and Watson north (no hills).

"You are all wrong," said Holmes. "We shall find him right in Eyford—and there's no doubt about what the gang is up to."

Which clue helped Holmes correctly locate Stark's place? What was Stark producing with the hydraulic press?

Across

1 Representatives: Abbr.
5 "Look ___ stars!"
10 Kind of fur
14 Like a pancake
15 "There's a long, long ___ . . ."
16 Woodwind
17 Albacore
18 ___ of a different color
19 German industrial region
20 Lover of beauty
22 Properly
24 Hebrides island
25 Encloses
26 Mummers
29 Indicating
33 "Bowed by the weight of centuries he ___ . . ."
34 Jogs
35 ___ Canals
36 Law degree

37 Devises
38 "All ___ one . . ."
39 Bullfight cry
40 Jail: Slang
41 Nasal tone
43 Warbled
45 Rough
46 City in Spain
47 Free: Ger.
48 Degrade
51 Covered with icing
54 Actor Guinness
55 Actress Terry
57 Not have the remotest ___
59 Argot
60 Landlord's contract
61 Feminine nickname
62 Partner of odds
63 Members of Hindu sect
64 Strain at a ___

Down

1 Astern
2 Adhesive
3 Light browns
4 ___ wagon
5 Capital of Greece
6 Trout: It.
7 Biblical weed
8 "All ___ faults observ'd . . ."
9 The ___ (wind, rain, etc.)
10 Woodland
11 Border on
12 Eastern eye makeup
13 Weird
21 ___ d'oeuvre
23 Son of Seth
25 Large flower
26 Brass, for example
27 Stringed instrument
28 Domesticated
29 Dehydrated

30 "Peace to him that ___ off . . ."
31 Middays
32 Ravine
34 By the same ___.
37 Honorary Kentucky titles
40 Entreaty
41 "The Pobble who has no ___ . . ."
42 Kind of list
44 Chooses
45 Hags
47 Unwithered
48 Freshwater fish
49 Verve
50 Repair
51 Antiaircraft fire
52 ". . . a garden eastward in ___."
53 Walter ___ Mare, English poet
56 Hawaiian wreath
58 Height: Abbr.

Puzzle VI:
The Adventure of the Engineer's Thumb

Solution and epilogue on page 145

___ ___ ___ ___ ___ ___ , ___ ___ ___ ___ ___ ___ ___ ___

37 Down   18 Across   42 Down

___ ___ ___ ___ ___ ___ ___ ___ ___ ___ ___ ___ ___ ___ ___.

5 Across   4 Down   47 Down

___ ___ ___ ___ ___ ___ ___ ___ ___ ___ ___ ___ ___ ___ ___.

26 Down   38 Across   10 Across   37 Across

The Scotland Yarders

*P*In the beginning the unwritten compact between Sherlock Holmes and the Scotland Yarders could hardly have been called an *entente cordiale*. Scorn and derision abounded on the part of Holmes, mistrust and misunderstanding on the Yarders' side.

Said Holmes in amused indignation about one of his callers, "Fancy his having the insolence to confound me with the official detective force!"

But the suspicious, leery Scotland Yarders found little to smile about.

"I've heard of your methods . . . Mr. Holmes. You are ready enough to use all the information that the police can lay at your disposal, and then you try to finish the case yourself and bring discredit upon them." So said "foxy" Forbes, Yard detective.

But even so, the Scotland Yarders loom large in the Holmes chronicles. They were involved in or mentioned in more than half of Holmes's adventures because they and Holmes needed each other: the unofficial sleuth who abhorred inaction was often saved from dying of ennui, when things were slow, by the cases that the baffled Yarders brought him.

"The pick of a bad lot," Holmes was quick to tell Watson, when Inspectors G. Lestrade (could it be Gustave?) and Tobias Gregson turned up in *A Study in Scarlet*, the first of the Holmes adventures. Lestrade was also the first of the Yarders to make the grudging pilgrimage to Baker Street. "He got himself into a fog recently over a forgery case, and that was what brought him here," explained Holmes, and "in a fog" might have been the title of the Scotland Yarders' theme song as they blundered their way through the stories.

"That imbecile Lestrade," who appeared in more of the tales than any other Yarder, was a "little sallow, rat-faced, dark-eyed fellow" who thoroughly disapproved of Holmes's methods. "I am afraid, Holmes, that you are not very practical with your deductions and your inferences," was the inspector's sneering comment. "I believe in hard work, and not in sitting by the fire spinning fine theories."

And to Inspector Lestrade's credit, it must be said that he did work hard. But he was a dull boy, who usually jumped quickly to the wrong conclusion. This sad failing, which Lestrade shared with the other Scotland Yarders, became apparent early on in *A Study in Scarlet*. Lestrade had diligently searched the scene of the murder, a room in a dark deserted house, and had found the word "Rache" written in letters of blood on a wall.

"You mark my words," he prognosticated, "when this case comes to be cleared up, you will find that a woman named Rachel has something to do with it. It's all very well for you to laugh, Mr. Sherlock Holmes. You may be very smart and clever, but the old hound is the best, when all is said and done."

Watson, Holmes, and "foxy" Forbes.

" 'Rache' is the German for 'revenge'," said Holmes coldly, "so don't lose your time looking for Miss Rachel."

Lestrade and Gregson and the other Scotland Yarders asked for and accepted the brilliant consultant's help with mixed emotions: disdainfully, resentfully, gratefully, at times in awe. Holmes was always glad to give his help, but frequently it was given together with a good dose of sarcasm. "Yes, Lestrade, I congratulate you! With your usual happy mixture of cunning and audacity, you have got him."

At the back of the professionals' minds was the constant, gnawing worry that Holmes would garner the glory. More than once Holmes had had to explain, as he did to foxy Forbes when that angry man had accused him, that this was not the way he worked. It was Holmes's habit to give credit to the Scotland Yard detective for untangling a case in which they both were involved, and which Holmes, of course, had solved. As he told Watson, "When Gregson, or Lestrade, or Athelney Jones are out of their depths—which, by the way, is their normal state—the matter is laid before me. I claim no credit in such cases. The work itself . . . is my highest reward."

And so the newspapers paid due respect to the exceptional talents of the Scotland Yarders. Holmes enjoyed reading their misguided accounts. Here is the *Standard*, praising Athelney Jones:

The prompt and energetic action of the officers of the law shows the great advantage of the presence . . . of a single vigorous and masterful mind.

"Isn't it gorgeous!" Holmes would crow, but the good Watson was not amused by these distortions of the truth. He had made up his mind, as soon as he had heard about Holmes's arrangements with Scotland Yard, to set the record straight. "I have all the facts in my journal, and the public shall know them."

As time went by, the air between Holmes and the Scotland Yarders began to clear. Holmes was mellowing, and the Yarders had come to esteem the Master. Lestrade and Gregson and Jones had not perceptibly gained in intelligence or wit, but Holmes could find a positive quality or two: thoroughness, tenacity. No longer did he say that a motive was so transparent that even a Scotland Yard official could see through it. He could say of Lestrade, "He is the best of the professionals, I think, and we may need his assistance." And Watson could observe "the reverential way in which Lestrade gazed" at Holmes.

Finally, Holmes went so far as to adopt a protégé from Scotland Yard, a promising young inspector named Stanley Hopkins. The thirty-year-old Hopkins, "for whose future Holmes had high hopes," was a well-built, alert fellow, eager to learn. Hopkins was the closest thing to a son and heir that the confirmed bachelor Holmes was ever to have. But while Hopkins's admiration and respect for Holmes's scientific methods continued to grow, the great investigator's high hopes for his pupil slowly faded.

In "The Adventure of Black Peter," when the earnest Hopkins after a week of struggle on the murder case called at Baker Street to see Holmes, this unhappy dialogue took place:

"I know your methods, sir, and I applied them. Before I permitted anything to be moved, I examined most carefully the ground outside, and also the floor of the room. There were no footmarks."

"Meaning that you saw none?"

"I assure you, sir, that there were none."

"My good Hopkins, I have investigated many crimes, but I have never yet seen one which was committed by a flying creature."

"I am disappointed in Stanley Hopkins," Holmes confessed to Watson. In time, disappointment turned to resignation. Discussing Hopkins's last case, Holmes said of his protégé's misreading of the clues, "Well . . . I have given Hopkins an excellent hint, and if he can't avail himself of it I can do no more."

It was Lestrade, of all people, who gave Holmes one of his finest moments. In "The Adventure of the Six Napoleons," after Lestrade in his obtuse fashion had completely misunderstood all the events and overlooked all the clues, and Holmes had triumphantly solved the case, Lestrade expressed his own and Scotland Yard's genuine appreciation of Holmes's work: "If you come down tomorrow, there's not a man, from the oldest inspector to the youngest constable, who wouldn't be glad to shake you by the hand." Thanking Lestrade, Holmes turned away, and it seemed to Watson that "he was more nearly moved by the softer human emotions than I had ever seen him."

The Adventure of the Noble Bachelor

In the sitting room at Baker Street, Lord Robert St. Simon, son of the Duke of Balmoral, was discussing with Sherlock Holmes and Watson the mysterious disappearance of his bride a few days earlier. The foppishly dressed lord, high-nosed and pale, looking older than his forty-one years, was clearly a provoked man.

"I have been cut to the quick, Mr. Holmes," said he. "Scotland Yard is already acting in the matter, but Inspector Lestrade sees no objection to your cooperation. I understand you have managed several cases of this sort, sir, though I presume that they were hardly from the same class of society."

"No, I am descending. My last client of the sort was a king."

Before St. Simon's arrival, Holmes had gathered from the newspapers an account of the extraordinary events immediately following St. Simon's wedding. The lord had wed Miss Hatty Doran, beautiful young daughter of Aloysius Doran of San Francisco, a millionaire who had been a poor miner until he struck gold. And while Hatty was gaining a title, the marriage was also considered a fortunate one for the lord, who owned only a small estate.

The wedding, at St. George's, had been a small, quiet one; the party had returned for the wedding breakfast to Mr. Doran's rented house at Lancaster Gate. A disturbance had been caused by a Miss Flora Millar, formerly a *danseuse*, trying to force her way into the house, alleging she had a claim on St. Simon. She had been ejected, and was later arrested when the bride vanished.

The bride herself had sat down to breakfast with the rest of the party, but, suddenly declaring she felt ill, had gone to her room. It was later learned from her maid that Hatty had rushed in, donned an ulster over her wedding dress, and had hurried out. When she did not return, St. Simon had called in the police.

"I should like to know more about your wife, Lord St. Simon," said Holmes. "What is your own impression of her character?"

"My wife was twenty before her father became a rich man; during that time, motherless, she ran free in a mining camp. She is a tomboy, impetuous—but she is noble and honorable."

"Did you see Miss Doran the day before the wedding?"

"Yes, she was in good spirits, talking of our future. But there was a change next day, after the ceremony. An incident too trivial to relate upset her."

"Pray let us have it, for all that," said Holmes.

"She dropped her bouquet as we left the altar. It fell into the front pew, where a gentleman handed it up to her again. The bouquet was none the worse, but she was absurdly agitated."

"Some of the general public were present, then?"

"Yes, the church is open to all; the man was not known to us."

"What did Lady St. Simon do on reentering her father's house?"

"She spoke to her maid—said something about 'jumping a claim.' "

"And after she left the house, was she seen anywhere?"

"A footman saw her leave, but took her for a guest. She was then seen walking into Hyde Park with Flora Millar, but she did not know who Flora was—she'd gone in before the disturbance."

"Ah, Miss Millar. May I ask about your relations to her?"

St. Simon raised an eyebrow. "We have been on a *very* friendly footing for some years; I have treated her generously. But she is hot-headed, and was very angry when she learned I was to marry. Mr. Lestrade thinks Flora decoyed my wife and laid a trap for her, but Flora wouldn't hurt a fly."

"Why do you think your wife disappeared?"

"It may be that the consciousness of having made so immense a social stride has caused her to become nervously disturbed."

"A conceivable hypothesis," said Holmes, smiling. "From your seat at the breakfast table, could you see out the window?"

"We could see the other side of the road and the Park."

"I need detain you no longer. I have solved the problem."

"Eh, what was that? Where, then, is my wife?"

"That is a detail which I shall supply very soon."

Shortly after St. Simon's departure, a discouraged Inspector Lestrade came calling, carrying a black canvas bag. "This infernal case! We have been dragging the Serpentine all day in search of the body of Lady St. Simon—"

"In heaven's name, what for? You won't find the lady there!"

"Oh, indeed! We found this in it!" Lestrade opened his bag as he spoke; out tumbled Lady St. Simon's watery wedding dress. "And this note! Found in a card-case in one of the pockets of the dress. It implicates Miss Flora Millar! Listen to this: 'You will see me when all is ready. Come at once. F. H. M.' "

"Let me see it," said Holmes, as he took up the note. He gave a cry of satisfaction. "Ah, this is indeed important!"

"But you are looking at the wrong side!" shouted Lestrade.

"On the contrary, this is the right side. It's a fragment of a hotel bill; from the prices, one of the most select in London. I congratulate you, Lestrade!"

"I've wasted time enough!" said Lestrade, stalking out.

He had hardly shut the door behind him when Holmes put on his overcoat. "That note, Watson, will help clear up the matter sooner than I had hoped. Of course, I had formed my conclusion before St. Simon arrived: There is no Lady St. Simon."

"My dear Holmes! I can make neither head nor tail of this business, yet I have heard all that you have heard."

"Without, however, the knowledge of similar cases which serves me so well. In each a very like set of circumstances prevailed. I shall return soon, and make it all plain to you."

To what circumstances did Holmes refer? Without his knowledge, were you able to guess from the clues?

Across

1 College degrees
5 French priest
9 ____flam
13 Aleutian island
14 Hold in ____ (restrain)
16 Rajah's mate
17 Grease
18 African language
19 Publicizes
20 Small amounts
22 Hush-hush
24 ____ in print (comes out)
25 Canyon mouth
26 Seine
27 Commending
31 Temporize
34 Pine Tree State
35 More than enough
36 Compassion
37 ____ out (gave sparingly)

38 Mexican coin
39 Numero ____
40 ____ off (wipe dry)
41 Blundered
42 Gave an account of
44 Soul: Fr.
45 Kind of garden
46 Intend
50 Did away with
53 ". . . merry as a ____ bell."
54 Thought
55 Clerical vestment
57 Algerian seaport
58 Lath
59 Musical symbols
60 États-____
61 Dried up
62 Fling
63 Rational

Down

1 Light wood
2 Character
3 Anchor position
4 Unexpectedly
5 Victoria's beloved
6 Spill the ____ (blab)
7 Prohibits
8 Superlative suffix
9 Brawl
10 "Rouse the lion from his ____."
11 As to
12 "As the ____ resembles the rain."
15 Conserve
21 Celt
23 Pennsylvania port
25 Prospero's servant
27 Faded
28 Brain canal
29 Proboscis
30 Make ____ (succeed)

31 On the ____ of the moment
32 Prong
33 Sleep like ____
34 Grass cutter
37 Was fond of
38 Prior
40 Corner
41 Moslem noble
43 Flattened at the poles
44 Under ____ (in legal custody)
46 Valleys
47 ____ living (make one's way)
48 Encore!
49 Present, for example
50 "Or leave a ____ but in the cup . . ."
51 Loaf
52 Shakespearean king
53 Hari
56 Bird of fable

Puzzle VII:
The Adventure of the Noble Bachelor

A crossword grid with numbered squares.

Solution and epilogue on page 146

1) _ _ _ _ _ _ _ _ _   _ _ _ _ _ _ _

   38 Down   22 Across

_ _ _ _ _ _ _ _ .   2) _ _ _ _ _ _ _

53 Across   15 Down

_ _ _ _ _ _ _ _ _   _ _ _ _ _ _ _ .   3) _ _ _ _ -

42 Across   50 Across   15 Down

_ _ _   _ _ _ _ _ _ _ _   _ _ _ _ _ _ .

     4 Down   24 Across

The Adventure of the Beryl Coronet

Outside, on Baker Street, all was quiet in the early, frosty February morning; the pale sun glinted on the deep, crusted snow that had fallen the day before. But inside the sitting room of 221B, a violent scene was taking place. A middle-aged man, tall, imposing, had rushed into the room, and was beating his head against the wall with such force that it took both Sherlock Holmes and Dr. Watson to restrain him. When they had soothed the distraught man so that he could speak, he told of the terrible events that had brought him to such a pass.

"My name," said the man, "is probably familiar to you. I am Alexander Holder, senior partner of the banking firm of Holder & Stevenson. The police inspector suggested that I should secure your cooperation, Mr. Holmes; time is short!

"Yesterday one of England's highest nobles came to my office seeking a loan of £50,000 for four days, and bringing as security one of the empire's most precious public possessions—the Beryl Coronet, a dazzling sight, with thirty-nine enormous beryls set in gold. The stones are unique, irreplaceable; my client warned that any injury to the coronet would be as serious as its loss, causing the greatest public scandal. I granted the loan with misgivings, fearful for the safety of the jewel which had been placed in my keeping. When evening came I felt I could not leave it in the office—bankers' safes have been forced before. To make sure the coronet would be always within my reach, I brought it home and took it upstairs to my dressing-room, where I locked it in the bureau.

"And now a word as to my household. All of my servants but one have been with me many years, and all are absolutely reliable. Lucy Parr came a few months ago, with excellent references, but being pretty she attracts admirers who hang about.

"I am a widower with an only son, Arthur. He has been a grievous disappointment to me, Mr. Holmes. People tell me I have spoiled him; very likely. Under the influence of his friend, Sir George Burnwell, he is wayward, gambles heavily, and is often in debt. We have few visitors, but Sir George calls frequently, and I can understand his influence—he is handsome, brilliant, a man of the world, but he is not to be trusted. So think I, and so does my niece, Mary, my sunbeam, whom I adopted when my brother died. She is kind, beautiful, a wonderful housekeeper. Twice my boy has asked her to marry him—he loves her devotedly—but she has refused him.

"After dinner last night I told Arthur and Mary of the treasure we had under our roof, and where I had locked it.

" 'Any old key will fit that bureau,' Arthur said. But he has a wild way of talking, so I thought little of what he said. Later, he followed me upstairs to my room with a grave face.

" 'Dad, can you let me have £200 to settle a debt of honour?'

" 'No, I cannot! I have been far too generous with you!'

" 'I must raise the money in some way,' he said. 'If you will not let me have it, then I must try other means.'

" 'Not a farthing!' I cried. He left without another word.

"I started to go round the house to secure it—a duty which I usually leave to Mary. As I came down the stairs, I found her closing the side window of the hall, looking somewhat upset.

" 'Lucy did not have leave to go out tonight,' she said, 'but she came in just now by the back door. I shall speak to her.'

"Mary having assured me that everything was fastened, I went up to my bedroom again, and was soon asleep. About two in the morning I was awakened by some sound in the house, as though a window had gently closed. Then, to my horror, I heard footsteps moving in my dressing-room. I looked in, palpitating with fear.

" 'Arthur!' I screamed, 'you villain! you thief!'

"He stood barefoot, wearing only shirt and trousers, holding the coronet, which was twisted—he seemed to be wrenching at it. At my cry he dropped it and turned as pale as death. I snatched it up, *and then I saw that a gold corner with three beryls was missing!* He angrily refused to give any explanation.

" 'You shall learn nothing from me!' said he. 'If you choose to call the police, let the police find what they can.'

"By this time the whole house was astir. Mary was the first to rush in, and, at the sight of the coronet and of Arthur's face, with a scream she fell down senseless to the floor.

"I sent for the police. A search was made not only of Arthur's person but of his room, and of every place where he could possibly have concealed the gems. He was arrested, but he will not speak. The missing corner must be found, Mr. Holmes; spare no expense. I have lost my honour and my son in one night!"

Holmes sat silent for some few minutes, his brows knitted.

"You receive few visitors," he said, "but do you go out much?"

"Arthur does," replied Holder. "Mary and I stay at home."

"That is unusual in a young girl," observed Holmes.

"She is of a quiet nature, and not so young—twenty-four."

"I see." Holmes paused, then said briskly, "I think your son is not guilty, Mr. Holder. He would not have stayed in the dressing-room to be caught. We must find out why he is silent."

Holmes and Watson accompanied Mr. Holder back to his suburban home, a large square house. While his companions waited, Holmes made a survey round the house. In the back were stables, a garden, and paths, all blanketed with pristine snow except where footsteps had left their imprints. Going inside, they found an anguished Mary waiting. She was a tall, slim young woman, whose dark hair and eyes seemed even darker against the pallor of

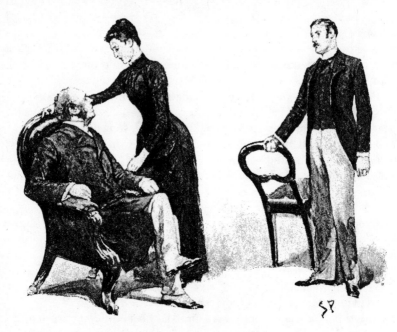

"She pleaded with her uncle."

her skin. She pleaded with her uncle to have Arthur released.

"He'll not be freed until the gems are found!" said Holder.

"Miss Holder," asked Holmes, "were the windows you fastened last night still all fastened this morning?" When she nodded, he continued, "You have a maid who has a sweetheart?"

"Yes—Lucy. She served the coffee last night, and so may have heard talk of the coronet. Her sweetheart is the greengrocer."

"And he is a man with a wooden leg?" Holmes added.

Something like fear sprang up in Mary's expressive eyes. "Why, you are like a magician," she said.

"I should like to go upstairs now," said Sherlock Holmes.

He inspected the bureau in the dressing-room, commenting on its noiseless lock. "That's why it didn't wake you, Mr. Holder."

Next he examined the beautiful diadem. "Try to break off a corner, Mr. Holder." The banker recoiled in horror. "Then I will." Holmes suddenly bent all his strength upon it, but without result. "It took more than one person to break it!"

Making ready to depart, Holmes told the banker, "I may have news for you soon. Please call on me tomorrow morning at ten."

Outside, Holmes remarked to Watson, "There were some interesting footprints in the snow back of the house—where a woman and a man with a wooden leg met, and where a barefoot man and a booted man scuffled." He would say no more.

Back at home Holmes disguised himself as a vagrant, and, apologizing to Watson, set out alone. He returned in two hours, in high spirits, carrying a pair of old boots.

"These fit the boot tracks exactly," he said. "I bought them from their owner's valet. Now, my dear Watson, I must go out again, this time as my own respectable self. Don't wait up."

Next morning Mr. Holder called at Baker Street in utter defeat, more painful to see than his violence of the day before.

"My niece, my Mary, has deserted me," he said. "I had said to her last night—in sorrow, Mr. Holmes, not in anger—if only she had married my boy. She left me this note. 'I have brought trouble upon you, and must leave forever. Do not worry; my future is provided for.' My God, does it point to suicide?"

"No, no, nothing of the kind," said Holmes. "It is perhaps the best possible solution. But now, Mr Holder, I have something for you—" and he took from his desk a triangular piece of gold with three large gems in it.

"I am saved!" shrieked the banker. "And England is saved from a terrible scandal! How did you do it, Mr. Holmes?"

"I have a maxim—when you have excluded the impossible, whatever remains, however improbable, must be the truth. Now, sir, you owe two things: the £3000 I had to pay to retrieve the gems, and a very humble apology to that noble lad, your son."

From the clues could you guess 1) who stole the coronet, 2) who got it from the thief, 3) who broke it? What then happened 4) to the coronet corner, 5) to Mary?

Across

1 One-celled animal
6 Louts
10 School subj.
14 Monkey's cousin
15 Aviated
16 Give _____ (punish)
17 Theological rationalist
18 Kind of district
20 21st U.S. president
22 Israeli seaport
23 Hindu title of address
24 Aphrodite's son
26 Radiate
28 Betrayals
32 Theatre sign
33 Poem by Horace
34 Actress Gwyn
36 Rage
40 Storyteller
42 Beauty-salon appliance

44 Largest continent
45 Jeans fabric
47 Being: Sp.
48 Swiss river
49 Lusterless
51 Cautiously
54 _____ and sevens (at odds)
58 Yours: Fr.
59 Personal pronoun
60 Hawaiian fish
62 Sink
66 Wrestling
69 Masculine name
70 French eye
71 Sioux
72 *Beau* _____
73 "_____ thy father, and refuse thy name . . ."
74 _____ through with (completed)
75 Tallinn is their capital

Down

1 Actor Robert or Alan
2 Jan van der _____, Dutch painter
3 Send out
4 Four pecks
5 Toscanini
6 At a distance
7 Inter _____
8 Parry
9 Throngs
10 _____ jacet (here lies)
11 "_____ far, far better thing . . ."
12 Commence
13 "He maketh me _____ down . . ."
19 Comes close
21 Spherical
25 Cubic meter
27 _____ bene
28 Dealt in
29 Feminine nickname
30 Incline
31 David's weapon

35 _____ go (forget it)
37 Gravel ridges
38 Iranian coin
39 Sister of Lazarus
41 "_____ , Pagliaccio . . . "
43 Go back on a promise
46 Snafu
50 Mature
52 New York lake
53 Endows
54 "Truth is as old _____ . . ."
55 Usual number of cheers
56 "They that go down to the _____ ships . . ."
57 Set of rooms
61 By and by
63 Fruit: Ger.
64 In the company of
65 Compass points
67 Single thickness
68 Acquire

Puzzle VIII:
The Adventure of the Beryl Coronet

Solution and epilogue on page 147

1) __ __ __ __ ,   2) __ __ __ __ __ __ __ ,   3) __ __ __ __ __ __ __ ,
  39 Down   52 Down   20 Across

__ __ __ __ __ __ __ ,   __ __ __ __ __ __ __ __ __ .
52 Down   66 Across

4) __ __ __ __ __ __   __ __ __ __   __ __   __ __   __ __ __ __ __ .
  52 Down   28 Down   16 Across   8 Down

5) __ __ __   __ __ __ __   __ __ __   __ __ __ __   __ __ __ __ __ .
  59 Across   74 Across   6 Down   64 Down   52 Down

Silver Blaze

The disappearance of Colonel Ross's horse, Silver Blaze, the favorite for the Wessex Cup, occurring at the same time as the murder of its trainer, John Straker, a week before the race, was the talk of England. Both Ross and Inspector Gregory, who was acting on the case, had sent telegrams to Sherlock Holmes, inviting his cooperation, and Holmes, who had read the newspaper accounts with the keenest interest, accepted eagerly. So it was that he and Watson were soon on the train to Dartmoor where King's Pyland, the colonel's training stable, was situated.

"Have you formed a theory?" asked Watson, who had observed Holmes devouring the morning papers he had brought with him.

"I have a grip on the essential facts," said Holmes. "As you know, enormous sums have been laid on the favorite, so Ross had taken every precaution to guard Silver Blaze. He stabled only four horses; Straker had three lads working for him—one sat up each night in the stable, while the others slept in the loft.

"John Straker, who was married, lived in a house a short distance from the stable. About a half mile to the north is a small cluster of villas. To the west, about two miles across the moor, is the larger, rival training stable of Mapleton, managed by Silas Brown. And round all is the wild moor.

"On the fatal night, two lads supped at Straker's; the third, Ned Hunter, remained on guard. As the maid was bringing Hunter's supper of curried mutton to the stable, she was waylaid by a well-dressed stranger, who carried a heavy stick. He wanted her to slip Hunter a folded piece of white paper. Frightened, she ran past him to the small stable window and handed in the dish to Hunter. The man followed, and spoke to the lad at the window.

" 'You've two horses in the Wessex Cup—Silver Blaze and Bayard. Let me have the straight tip; you won't be the loser.'

" 'So, you're a damned tout!' cried Hunter. He ran across the stable to unloose the dog; the maid fled, but looking back saw the man poking his head through the window. Hunter locked the door and rushed out with the dog; the man had disappeared.

"Straker was excited at hearing of the incident; his wife, waking at one in the morning, found him with his coat on, ready to go to the stables to see that all was well, although a storm had come up. In the morning, alarmed that John had not returned, Mrs. Straker went with the maid to the stables. The door was open; Hunter was in a state of stupor; Silver Blaze was gone.

"A search turned up Straker's coat, flapping from a bush, a quarter-mile from the stable. Immediately beyond was a depression in the moor, in which lay Straker's body. His head had been crushed by a heavy weapon, and his thigh was slashed. In his right hand was a knife clotted with blood; in his left a red cravat, recognized by the maid as having been worn by the tout. Silver

Blaze's footsteps were found in the mud at the bottom of the hollow. Analysis of the remains of Hunter's meal showed a large amount of powdered opium. Hunter would surely have detected its distinct taste had it not been masked by the curry.

"Inspector Gregory at once found and arrested the tout, one Fitzroy Simpson; he lives in the small cluster of villas. He did not deny his actions, but said he had only wanted information—the white paper was a ten-pound note. When shown his cravat he turned pale and said he had lost it. His wet clothes proved he had been out in the storm, and his leaded stick could easily have caused Straker's injuries. But—interestingly—though Straker's knife was clotted with blood, Simpson had no wound on his person."

"Straker may have fallen on his own knife," said Watson.

"Excellent!" cried Holmes. "The police have it that Simpson drugged Hunter's food through the window, entered the stable with a duplicate key, bridled Silver Blaze, and was with him on the moor when Straker overtook them. The tout killed Straker, secreted Silver Blaze somewhere, or the horse bolted and is now loose on the moor."

Inspector Gregory, a tall, fair man, and Colonel Ross, a small, dapper one, were waiting at the station when Holmes and Watson arrived. They were soon on their way to Straker's house.

"I've examined every stable within a radius of ten miles," said Gregory. "Not a sign of Silver Blaze. Silas Brown, the trainer at Mapleton, is known to have large bets on their horse, Desborough, but there's nothing to connect him with the affair, and nothing to connect Simpson with the Mapleton interests."

At Straker's home, Holmes examined the items recovered from the trainer's pockets, which he found of singular interest: a box of matches, two inches of candle, and a Bond Street bill for a very expensive dress made out to William Derbyshire. Mrs. Straker, a thin, drawn woman, said Derbyshire was a friend of her husband's whose mail often came to their home. Holmes also examined the knife that had been found in Straker's hand; his wife said he had picked it up from the table on his way to the stable.

"If I am not mistaken, Watson, this is a surgical knife."

"Yes," said Watson, "a cataract knife, for very delicate work."

"A strange weapon for a rough expedition," observed Holmes.

The men left the Straker home for the scene of the crime.

"I understand there was no wind that night," said Holmes, "so Straker's coat was not blown against the bush, but placed there." Gregory nodded. Holmes went down into the hollow, where he made a careful study, and picked up a half-burnt match from the mud.

"I can't think how I overlooked it," said Gregory, annoyed.

"I only saw it because I was looking for it," said Holmes.

Colonel Ross, impatient with Holmes's methods, asked Gregory to go along with him to withdraw his horse's name from the race.

"A surly Silas Brown turned ashy white."

"No, no," cried Holmes. "I should let it stand."

Before Gregory left, he gave Holmes a cast horseshoe of Silver Blaze. "I'll put it in my pocket for luck," said Holmes.

Holmes and Watson walked across the moor towards Mapleton.

"Horses are gregarious," said Holmes. "A working hypothesis: If Blaze bolted, he'd have gone home or to Mapleton. There may be tracks in the mud. Aha!" They had come upon a horse's track heading for Mapleton; Blaze's horseshoe fitted it exactly. Farther on, a man's tracks joined the horse's. The double track turned round towards King's Pyland, then turned back again.

As they reached Mapleton, Holmes said, "I shall tell Silas Brown that I know he has Silver Blaze. He has colored the white spot on Blaze's forehead—that's why Gregory didn't find him."

A surly Silas Brown turned ashy white when Holmes confronted him. Holmes instructed him not to produce Blaze until the day of the race. Walking back to Straker's, Holmes explained to Watson, "Ross has been a trifle cavalier to me. I am having a little amusement at his expense. Say nothing about the horse."

Ross and Gregory were awaiting them in the parlor.

"We are returning to London on the night train," said Holmes.

"So you despair of finding Straker's murderer," Ross sneered.

Holmes shrugged. "I have some matters to look into on Bond Street. I hope your horse will start; have your jockey ready. Might I ask for a photograph of Mr. John Straker?"

He was given the photograph, and as Holmes and Watson were on the way to their carriage, Holmes asked one of the stableboys, "Have you noticed anything amiss with the sheep you keep here?"

"Not of much account, but three of them have gone lame, sir."

"Ah," said Holmes. "Take note, Gregory; that is important."

"Anything else you wish to draw to my attention, Mr. Holmes?"

"The curious incident of the stable dog in the nighttime."

"The dog did nothing in the nighttime."

"That was the curious incident," said Sherlock Holmes.

On race day Holmes and Watson drove with Ross to the course.

"I have seen nothing of my horse," said Ross coldly. "We have scratched the other one, and put our hopes on your word."

The last horse out of the weighing enclosure cantered past, the jockey wearing the colonel's black and red colors.

"That's not my horse!" cried Ross. "Not a white hair on him!"

"You have only to wash his face in spirits of wine, and you will find he is the same as ever," said Holmes.

Silver Blaze won handily. In the weighing enclosure, patting his horse, Ross turned to Holmes and said, "I owe you an apology. You've done me a great service. It would be greater still if you could lay your hands on the murderer of poor John Straker."

"I have," said Holmes quietly. "He is standing behind you."

Who killed John Straker? What circumstances brought about his death? From the clues, could you guess?

Across

1 Mr. Doe
5 Frizzle
10 Flying jib, for example
14 Lily genus
15 Steamship
16 Feminine name
17 "As I _____ St. Ives . . ."
19 Appear on the horizon
20 Slandered
21 Raise
23 Kind of ear
24 Irritate
25 Arctic Ocean sea
29 Originals
33 Sly look
34 Helen of Troy's abductor
37 Mauna _____
38 King of Judah, et al.
39 Souvenir

40 Sharp: Fr.
41 _____zag
42 Yellow-fever mosquito
43 _____-do-well
44 Builds
46 Kind of Spanish grass
49 Kirghiz mountain range
51 Share: Slang
52 Wagering
55 Of the dawn
59 _____ the Red, discoverer of Greenland
60 Lead a _____ (deceive)
62 In the chips
63 Actress Barrymore
64 Footnote word
65 Suburb of Paris
66 Prescribed quantities
67 *Thin Man* dog

Down

1 Chins
2 Universe: Heb.
3 Flexible water pipe
4 Deniers
5 Customer
6 Peel
7 Participle ending
8 Measuring apparatus
9 Fertile
10 " . . . precious stone set in
the _____ sea . . ."
11 Celebes ox
12 "_____ Rhythm"
13 Kind of excuse
18 O'Neill character
22 Olympia's country
25 Burn brightly
26 Chief Norse gods
27 Reacts, in Rouen
28 Whizzed

30 More underhanded
31 "A time _____, and a time to lose . . ."
32 Lizard: Comb. form
35 Porter's relative
36 Partner of shine
39 Smoothed again with abrasive
40 Asian Turkey
42 Mythic king of the Huns
45 Tricky
47 Oared racing boats
48 "Blessed are the _____ in heart . . ."
50 "_____ prepare a place for you."
52 Half of a nutritional disease
53 Greek goddess of discord
54 Twitches
55 Have _____ in one's bonnet
56 Eve was made from one of these
57 Throw _____ (carry on)
58 Mother of Helen of Troy
61 Vocalized pauses

Puzzle IX: *Silver Blaze*

Solution and epilogue on page 148

__ __ __ __ __   __ __ __ __ __. __ __ __ __   __ __ __ __   __

10 Down   25 Down   1 Across   58 Down

__ __ __ __ __ __   __ __ __ __ ; __ __   __ __ __   __ __ __ __ __

60 Across   31 Down   62 Across

__ __ __ __ __ __ __ __ ,   __ __ __   __ __ __ __ __ __   __ __

52 Across   17 Across

__ __ __   __ __ __ __ __   __ __ __ __ .

51 Across   25 Down   13 Down

65

The Stockbroker's Clerk

In a first-class carriage on the Saturday train to Birmingham were Sherlock Holmes, Dr. Watson and Mr. Hall Pycroft. "Please tell your story to Dr. Watson, as you told it to me," said Holmes.

Pycroft, a young fellow with an honest face, in a top-hat and a black suit, looked just like what he was—a stockbroker's clerk.

"The worst of it," said he, "is that it shows me such a fool! I'd been at Coxon's five years, when they came a cropper, and all the clerks were turned out. Old Coxon gave me a ripping testimonial, but I was fairly desperate when I saw an advertisement of Mawson's, the richest house in London—to be answered by letter only. Back came their reply—if I'd appear next Monday I might start at once, at a pound a week, provided my appearance was satisfactory. No one knows how these things work. Some say the manager just plunges his hand in the heap, and pulls one out.

"The very next evening my landlady brought up the card of 'Arthur Pinner, Financial Agent,' and in walked a short, dark-haired, dark-eyed, black-bearded man, with a brisk way about him.

" 'Mr. Pycroft,' he said, 'you were engaged at Coxon's and are about to start at Mawson's. I heard of your great financial ability from Parker, who used to be Coxon's manager. Have you kept in touch with the market? May I test you? How are Ayrshires?'

" 'A hundred six and a quarter to a hundred five and a half.'

" 'Wonderful!' he cried. 'You are too good to be a clerk! By Monday you will be business manager of Franco-Midland Hardware Company, with a hundred branches in France. You've probably never heard of it because the capital was privately subscribed. My brother, Harry, is director; he asked me to find a good man. So, on Parker's word, we offer five hundred a year.'

" 'Five hundred!' I shouted. 'But, Mr. Pinner, I must be frank; Mawson is safe, and I know so little about your company—'

" 'Ah, smart!' he cried. 'Here's a hundred pounds in advance. Be in Birmingham tomorrow at one. And here's a note to my brother at our temporary offices. Now, write for me, "I shall act as business manager to Franco-Midland Hardware Company for £500."'

"I did as he asked, and he put the paper in his pocket.

" 'One other thing,' he said. 'What about Mawson's?'

" 'I'll write and resign,' said I.

" 'Well,' said he, 'I had a row over you with Mawson's manager. I went to ask him about you; he accused me of coaxing you away. I said I'd lay a fiver that when you had my offer he'd never hear from you again. He said he had picked you out of the gutter—you would not leave. His very words.'

" 'The scoundrel!' I cried. 'I shall certainly not write!'

"The next day I was off to Birmingham, and at the address at one, but could find no Franco-Midland Hardware Company. Then a chap came up and spoke to me. He was very like Arthur Pinner, same figure and voice, but he was shaven and had light hair.

" 'Mr. Pycroft?' he asked. 'I had a laudatory note from my brother this morning. I'm sorry we do not have our name up yet.'

"He took me upstairs to two dusty rooms; one had two chairs and a table, the other was empty. He must have noticed my disappointment, for he said, 'Rome wasn't built in a day, Mr. Pycroft. While we are in Birmingham, you are to list all hardware sellers in this Paris directory. Please take it with you.'

"I went back to my hotel, very uneasy. I brought in parts of the list every other day. But yesterday I noticed something that gave me a start—Harry Pinner had the same gold tooth on the left-hand side as had his brother! When I put that with the figure and voice being the same, and only those things altered which might be changed by a razor or a wig, I came to see Mr. Holmes."

"Intriguing, Watson, is it not?" said Holmes, with satisfaction. "We're going to play Mr. Pycroft's friends needing berths."

That evening, as they were walking towards the company's offices, Pycroft said, "There he is." They watched as Pinner bought the late edition of the newspaper, and shortly after he entered the building they followed. In the first room they found him seated at the table, the paper spread out in front of him, and a look of the utmost horror and grief on his face.

"You look ill!" exclaimed Pycroft. Pinner made an effort to pull himself together, and listened as Pycroft explained their mission, but suddenly he cried out, "For God's sake, leave me!" Then he apologized, went into the next room, and closed the door.

"What now?" whispered Holmes. "Is he giving us the slip?"

"Impossible," said Pycroft. "There's no exit in that room."

After a few minutes they heard a sharp rat-tat from the inner room, followed by a low gargling sound. Holmes sprang at the closed door; it was locked, but the three men crashed it down. On a closet door, with his braces round his neck, his head at a dreadful angle, his heels clacking, hung Pinner. They took him down; Watson attended to him. "He'll live," said Watson.

"It's a mystery!" cried Pycroft. "Why did they want me—"

"Pooh," said Holmes. "It's all clear; I just don't understand this last move. It all hinges on three points. The first is making you write a declaration by which you entered the service of Franco-Midland. This is usually verbal. The second point is Pinner's influencing you not to resign your place, thus leaving Mawson's manager to expect you to report on Monday. Third is Pinner's playing two roles—obviously to free an accomplice for the mischief afoot. But why did Pinner try to hang himself?"

"The newspaper," croaked the voice of Pinner.

1) What did Pinner want Pycroft's note for? 2) Why did he stop Pycroft's resignation from Mawson's? 3) Who was Pinner's accomplice? 4) What were they after? 5) What was the newspaper headline?

Across

1 Position
6 "And one man ____ time plays . . ."
11 "An angel ____ in a book of gold."
13 Take up an occupation
15 Boat race
16 Sleepyheads
18 Actress Gardner
19 Unknown person
21 Suffix meaning "like"
22 Interjections of mild rebuke
24 Bishop's headdress
25 Highway: Abbr.
26 Cads
28 Scottish negative
29 Hard row ____
31 "My heart ____ . . . "
33 Candles
34 Aristocrats of Czarist Russia
36 Patisserie
37 Drunkards
38 More ironic
39 Superfluities
40 The way: Chin.
41 Bigwig
45 "My face is my fortune, ____ . . ."
46 Unwilling
48 Serum: Comb. form
49 Chemical suffix
50 Parader
52 Greek god of fields and forests
53 Animal chains
55 ____ Isle
57 Strong beer: Brit. Slang
58 Sells individually
59 Burros
60 ". . . a strength to the ____ in his distress."

Down

1 Trailer
2 Tie with surgical thread
3 ____ loss (puzzled)
4 Townspeople
5 Study of insects: Abbr.
6 Disregard
7 Not anybody
8 Animal skin
9 Hoosier State: Abbr.
10 " . . . and a star to ____ by . . ."
11 Fury
12 Saucy girls
14 Art of public speaking
17 Cuts
20 Greek letters
23 Killer
27 Cicatrices
29 ____ for (regarded as)
30 *Parsifal* and *Norma*
32 Time divisions: Abbr.
33 Siamese
34 Cow, ox, etc.
35 *Show Boat*, for example
36 "I am a ____ to dragons . . ."
37 "That I was ever born ____ it right!"
38 Part of British armed forces
40 Human trunks
42 "So attention must ____."
43 Viva voce
44 Fetters
46 Sweater size
47 Machos
50 ". . . fortune and ____ eyes . . ."
51 Network
54 Pronoun
56 Feminine name

Puzzle X: *The Stockbroker's Clerk*

Solution and epilogue on page 149

1) __ __ __ __ __ __ __ __ __ __ __ __.
   54 Down   11 Across

2) __ __ __ __ __
   37 Down

__ __ __ __ __ __ __ __ __ __ __ __ __ __ __ __ __ __ __ __ __.
19 Across   6 Across   1 Across

3) __ __ __ __ __ __ __ __ __ __.
   54 Down   36 Down

4) __ __ __ __ __ __.
   44 Down

5) __ __ __ __ __ __ __ __ __ __ __.
   23 Down   29 Down

69

The Reigate Puzzle

It was spring, but Sherlock Holmes, having worked unceasingly the past two months, was on the edge of nervous prostration. Watson had urged him to rest, and was delighted when Holmes accepted the invitation extended to them by Watson's old friend, Colonel Hayter, for a stay at his country home near Reigate.

On the evening of their arrival they were sitting in Hayter's gun-room after dinner when the colonel remarked, "I think I'll take a pistol upstairs with me—we have had a scare in these parts lately. Old Acton, one of our county magnates, had his house broken into last Monday; the fellows are still at large. It was a queer job—the whole place was turned upside down and ransacked, but all they took were Pope's *Homer*, two candlesticks, a letter-weight, a barometer, and a ball of twine."

"They were after something they couldn't find," said Holmes, "and took those things to make it appear an ordinary burglary."

"You're here for a rest," warned Watson. "Don't get started on a new problem." But his professional caution was wasted, for the next morning Hayter's butler rushed in with shocking news.

"Murder!" he gasped. "At the Cunninghams', sir."

"By Jove!" said Hayter. "Who's killed, the J. P. or his son?"

"Neither, sir. It was William, the coachman. Shot through the heart last night by a burglar—protecting his master's property. The thief never got a thing, but poor William died instantly."

"Curious," said Holmes. "I should think this is the last parish in England to which thieves would give attention."

"I fancy it's a local man," said Hayter. "You see, Acton's and Cunningham's are the largest places about here." Then he added, "But not the richest. They've had a lawsuit for some years; it's sucked the blood out of them. Old Acton has a claim on half of old Cunningham's estate, and the lawyers—"

They were interrupted by the arrival of Inspector Forrester. "We hear that Mr. Sherlock Holmes is here," he said eagerly.

"The fates are against you, Watson," said Holmes, laughing. "Perhaps you can let us have a few details, Inspector."

"We'd no clues in the Acton affair, but here the man was seen—by Mr. Cunningham from his bedroom window, and by his son Alec from the back passage. The alarm broke out at a quarter to twelve. Mr. Cunningham had just got into bed, and Mr. Alec was smoking a pipe in his dressing-gown. Both heard William calling for help, and Mr. Alec ran down. The back door was open, and he saw two men wrestling together outside. One of them fired a shot, and as the other dropped, the murderer fled instantly across the garden, through the hedge. Mr. Alec stopped to try to help William, so the villain got clean away. The robber must have just burst open the door—the lock had been forced—when William came upon him. We did get something important, though. Look at this."

He took a small piece of torn paper from a notebook.

"This was found between the finger and thumb of the dead man. It's a fragment from a larger sheet, reading as though it were an appointment. Perhaps William, though he was reputed to be honest, was in league with the thief, and they fell out."

Holmes took up the scrap of paper, which is here reproduced.

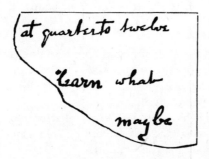

"This writing is of extraordinary interest!" he said. "It was obviously written by two persons! Look at the strong t's of 'at' and 'to' and the weak ones of 'quarter' and 'twelve.' One of the men distrusted the other and determined that each should have an equal hand in it. I should like to have a quiet glance into the details of this case. Colonel, I will leave my friend Watson and you, and step round with the Inspector."

An hour later Holmes and the inspector returned to ask Watson and Hayter to accompany them to the Cunningham home. On the way, Hayter asked if Holmes had visited the scene of the crime.

"We saw the body of the unfortunate man," said Holmes, "at the cottage where he lived with his mother. He surely died from a revolver wound as reported, but there was no powder-blackening on the clothes. Curious. Also, we saw the exact spot where the murderer went through the hedge—but at that point there is a moist ditch, and there were no boot-marks. The Inspector and I are agreed that the scrap of paper, bearing the very hour of William's death, is of great importance. Whoever wrote that note brought William to his death. But where's the rest of the sheet?"

"I looked for it very carefully, but—" said the inspector.

"It was torn out of the dead man's hand, because it was incriminating! And what would the villain do with it? Thrust it in his pocket, not noticing the missing corner. But if the assailant fled instantly, as you say, Inspector, then how could he have torn it from the dead man's hand?"

They had arrived at the Cunningham manor. Approaching, they saw two men come down the garden path; one was elderly, with a lined, heavy-eyed face, the other was a dashing young fellow.

"Still at it, Mr. Holmes?" asked young Alec Cunningham. "I don't see that we have any clues at all."

"There is one, if—Heavens, Mr. Holmes!" cried Forrester.

Holmes, his features writhing in agony, had fallen to the ground. Horrified by the attack, they carried him inside. He soon revived, however, and apologized. "Dr. Watson will tell you I am liable just now to these nervous attacks. But since I am here, I should like to verify a point. You were both in your rooms when William cried out—were your lamps lit? They were? Isn't it strange that a burglar should break into a house when he could see from the lights that the family were afoot?"

"He must have been a cool hand," said Alec Cunningham.

"What do you suggest we do, Mr. Holmes?" asked old Cunningham.

"I should like you to offer a reward," said Holmes. "I have jotted down the form here, if you don't mind signing it."

"This is wrong," said the J. P. "You wrote 'quarter to one,' but it was at a quarter to twelve that the attack was made." The old man corrected the mistake and handed the paper back to Holmes.

"Fine!" said Holmes, glancing at it with satisfaction. "Now, let's go over the house to make sure that nothing was stolen.

They all went up to the first floor of the house.

"I should like to see the view from the bedroom windows," said Holmes. "This is your son's bedroom?"—he opened the door—"and that is the dressing-room in which he was smoking when the alarm was given." Holmes glanced quickly around both rooms.

The J. P. led the way into his own chamber. As they all moved across it toward the window, Holmes fell back until he and Watson were the last in the group. On a table stood a dish of oranges and a carafe of water. Holmes leaned over and knocked the whole thing down. The glass smashed, and the fruit rolled all about.

"You've done it now, Watson," said Holmes coolly.

Watson understood that Holmes wanted him to take the blame, and began to pick up the fruit. The others did the same.

"Hullo!" cried the inspector. "Where's he got to?"

Holmes had disappeared.

"Wait here an instant," said Alec Cunningham. "The fellow is mad, in my opinion. Come, father, let's see where he's gone!"

They rushed from the room, leaving the inspector, the colonel, and Watson staring at each other.

Suddenly there was a scream of "Help! Help! Murder!" It was Holmes's voice. The three men ran into Alec's dressing-room, from which the voice had come. The Cunninghams were bending over the prostrate figure of

Holmes, the younger clutching his throat with both hands, while the elder seemed to be twisting his wrist. In an instant Watson and the inspector had torn them away from him, and Holmes staggered to his feet, very pale.

"Arrest these men for the murder of William," he gasped.

"I have no alternative, Mr. Cunningham," said Forrester. "It may all be a mistake—Ah, would you? Drop it!" He struck out, and the revolver in Alec's hand clattered to the floor.

"Keep that," said Holmes, putting his foot on it. "You will find it useful at the trial. But this is what we really wanted." He held up a little crumpled piece of paper.

"The rest of the sheet!" cried Forrester. "Where was it?"

"Where I was sure it would be—in Mr. Alec's dressing-gown."

Holmes deduced from the Cunninghams' report of the murder and from the note scrap that they had killed William, but he didn't know the motive until old Cunningham confessed. 1) What were Holmes's clues? 2) Can you outdo Holmes and guess the motive?

"*Bending over the prostrate figure of Holmes.*"

Across

1 Shed, as feathers
5 Old Russian Parliament
9 Hungarian wine
14 Bowfin genus
15 Smart ____
16 Man's nickname
17 Musical notation for guitar
19 Dropsy
20 London borough
21 Tangle in a net
22 Nimbuses
23 ____ bargain (seal a deal)
25 ____ off (canceling a debt)
28 Dozes
32 Eisenhower, et al.
35 Observe: Sp.
36 Alone
37 ____ over (redecorated)
38 Pickles: Sp.
39 "No, 'tis ____ so deep as a well . . ."
40 Pitcher
42 Mount ____
43 Kennedy and Williams
44 Pit
45 Heckler
47 Kind of steak
49 Semidiameters
53 Statement
56 Cripplers
58 Idolize
59 Extortion
61 Data
62 Orient
63 End: Ger.
64 He wrote "Mending Wall"
65 Heed
66 "____ we forget . . ."

Down

1 Kind of point, as in tennis
2 City in Nebraska
3 Defamation
4 Candle fats
5 Kind of line
6 Hawaiian fish
7 Mal de ____
8 Rickenbacker, for example
9 Join end ____ (butt)
10 "Her beauty was sold for an ____ gold . . ."
11 Swiss painter
12 Intentions
13 Uh-huh
18 Part of the Soviet Union: Abbr.
21 Indent in curved lines
23 ____ head off (snapped at)
24 ____ way (far gone)
26 Angry
27 West Indian birds
29 First-class
30 Trudge
31 Dipsomaniacs
32 Same: L.
33 Flightless bird
34 Paradise
41 Vacationlands
43 Shackle
46 French composer Satie
48 Extract by force
50 Silas ____ , American Revolutionary patriot
51 Crocuses
52 Ait
53 Rabble
54 Indian state
55 Somewhat: Music
56 Spar
57 Entr' ____ (intermission)
59 "O rare ____ Jonson!"
60 Buddhist Thai

Puzzle XI: *The Reigate Puzzle*

Solution and epilogue on page 150

1) __ __ __ __ __, __ __ __ __ __ __ __ __’ __ __ __ __ __ __ __ __ __ __ __
    15 Across   10 Down   53 Across   37 Across

__ __ __ __ __ __ __ __ __ __ __ __ __ __ __ __ __ __; __ __ __ __ __ __ __ __’__
39 Across   1 Down   61 Across   10 Down

__ __ __ __ __ __ __ __ __ __ __ __ __ __ __ __ __ __ __ __ __ __ __.
25 Across   37 Across   1 Down   65 Across

2) __ __ __ __ __ __ __ __ __ __ __ __ __ __ __ __.
    9 Down   59 Across

75

The Crooked Man

O ne summer midnight Sherlock Holmes rang the bell of the recently married Watson and asked to be put up for the night.

"With pleasure," said the astonished Watson. "Pray come in."

"Could you accompany me as a witness in a case I am about to clear up?" asked Holmes. "At the request of Major Murphy, of the Royal Munsters at Aldershot, I am assisting the police in their investigation of the slaying of Colonel James Barclay, commander of the famous regiment. Mrs. Barclay is under suspicion."

"I shall go gladly, but I've heard nothing of this murder."

"The facts are these," said Holmes. "The colonel married his wife thirty years ago in India, when he was a sergeant. She was Miss Nancy Devoy, the beautiful daughter of the color sergeant. The Barclays have lived at Aldershot many years; they were known as a model couple. As they had no children, Mrs. Barclay devoted herself to the charitable Guild of St. George. The colonel was a jovial man, but at times suffered strange fits of depression. The couple occupied a villa near the camp, thirty yards from the high-road, and employed a coachman, a cook, and a housemaid.

"On Monday night Mrs. Barclay attended a Guild meeting, in company of Miss Morrison, a neighbor. When Mrs. Barclay came home, she went to the morning-room, which faces the road and opens by a glass door on to the lawn—the blinds were not down. She asked Jane Stewart, the maid, to bring her a cup of tea, but when Miss Stewart returned, she heard the voices of the Barclays in the morning-room in furious altercation. She knocked, turned the handle, but the door was locked on the inside. She ran to fetch the cook and the coachman. They could hear Mrs. Barclay shouting, 'Coward! Give me back my life!' There was a dreadful cry from the colonel, a crash; Mrs. Barclay screamed. The coachman ran round to the lawn, and into the room. His mistress was insensible on a couch, while the colonel lay dead on the floor, his head in a pool of blood near a corner of the fender.

"Unable to find the door key, the coachman ran out the window to summon police and a doctor. The lady was removed to her room. A cut at the back of his head, evidently caused by a blunt weapon, had killed the colonel. Near the body was a club of hard wood with a bone handle, never before seen by the servants. The key was not found; a locksmith had to open the door.

"When I arrived yesterday morning I found that Mrs. Barclay was temporarily insane with brain fever. Everyone was speaking of the dreadful expression of horror on the dead man's face. But most important, I learned from Jane Stewart that twice during the quarrel Mrs. Barclay had spoken the word 'David!'

"The missing key indicated that a third person in the room had taken it. I found, indeed, that a man and a ferretlike creature, to judge from his footprints, had crossed the lawn coming from the road and entered the room.

"Mrs. Barclay had left home on good terms with her husband. Miss Morrison had been with her the whole time, but had said she had nothing to tell the police. When I visited Miss M., and told her that her friend might face a capital charge, she spoke out.

" 'We were on Hudson Street on our way home,' she said, 'when a bent, deformed man came towards us, carrying a box on his back.

" ' "My God, it's Nancy!" he screamed. She turned deathly white.

" ' "I thought you were dead these thirty years," she said.

" ' "So I have been," said he. He had a dark, fearsome face.

" 'Mrs. Barclay wanted a word with him, so I walked on a way. When she joined me, she begged me to tell no one of the matter.'

"I spent today, Watson, tracking the man down. He lives on Hudson Street, near the camp. His landlady said his name is Henry Wood; he is a conjurer and performer. He's only been there five days. He must have followed Mrs. Barclay home—he can tell us what happened in that room!"

Holmes and Watson arrived at Aldershot at midday, and called on Mr. Wood. The twisted man gave a violent start when Holmes told him that Mrs. Barclay would probably be tried for murder.

"You can take my word that she is innocent!" he cried.

"Then you are guilty," said Holmes.

"No, I am not. It was a just Providence that killed him! I am bent and ugly, but once Corporal Henry Wood was handsome. We were in India, Barclay and I, in the same company. We both loved Nancy, but she loved me. Her father wanted her to marry Barclay—he was educated—but I would have won had not the Mutiny broke out.

"Ten thousand rebels round us, and no water. I volunteered to warn General Neill of our danger—Barclay drew up my route. I was captured, tortured. I knew the native tongue, and learned that Barclay had betrayed me. After many years I escaped, a horrible cripple, shunning those I had known, wandering in India.

"When one gets old, one longs for home; I came here because I could earn my keep amusing the soldiers. I followed Nancy home, and saw the quarrel. My feelings overcame me; I broke in on them. Barclay died of guilt the moment he saw me, and fell with his head on the fender. Nancy fainted; I took the key from her hand, intending to get help, but then I thought things might look bad for me. I dropped my stick chasing my mongoose, who had got out of his box. If Nancy is in trouble, Mr. Holmes, I'll come forward."

"Thank you," said Holmes. "I hope it will not be necessary."

Walking on Hudson Street, Holmes and Watson met Major Murphy.

"The inquest has just proved death due to apoplexy," said Murphy. "A simple case, after all." Holmes, smiling, concurred.

As they left the major, Watson asked, "But whoever was David?"

Can you guess who David was, and why Mrs. Barclay spoke of him in her violent quarrel with her husband?

Across

1 Cigarette residues
6 Speech defect
10 Baron de _____, American patriot
14 *The Way of All* _____
15 Dazzler
16 Pelvic bones
17 California-Nevada lake
18 Business fall-off
20 Inlet
21 Strikes with wonder
23 Infuriated
24 Fireplace accessory
26 "It's the _____ the whole world over . . ."
27 Army V.I.P.
28 "But he who is _____ slain . . ."
32 _____ Camus, French writer
35 Record
36 "Age cannot wither _____ . . ."
37 Boo

38 Ribbed fabric
39 Kind of cobra
40 Navy V.I.P.
41 Cruising
43 Fast: Music
45 Scriptural
47 Gaelic sea god
48 "Madam, I'm _____."
49 Married man
53 Hunting dog
56 Experiment
57 _____ victis (woe to the vanquished)
58 Mother of Solomon
60 _____ all (mainly)
62 Islands of Indonesia
63 Mild oath
64 Tugged
65 Stitches
66 Small fishing boat
67 Facilitates

Down

1 TV-radio union
2 Put to death
3 "He gave to mis'ry all _____, a tear. . ."
4 That: Sp.
5 Fleecer
6 Actress Sophia
7 Senorita's name
8 Dry, as wine
9 Packaged houses
10 Fate
11 Et _____ (and others)
12 Celebrity
13 "Not with a _____ but a whimper."
19 Poison oak
22 Habit
25 "_____ no kick from champagne . . ."
26 Whippersnapper
28 Perfect
29 "_____ is the forest primeval."
30 _____ an ear (listened)
31 Therefore

32 Moby Dick's adversary
33 Italian city
34 Theatrical flop
38 Paper measure
39 Street edging: Brit.
41 Assistants
42 Excoriated
43 Over and above
44 Iterate
46 Eyelid fringes
49 Intoxicating
50 Declares
51 ". . . I am the Ruler of the Queen's _____!"
52 Feats
53 College degrees
54 Rhine tributary
55 Pack away
56 Ski-tow part
59 Part of the psyche
61 Neckpiece

Puzzle XII: *The Crooked Man*

Solution and epilogue on page 151

___ ___ ___ ___ ___ ___ ___.   ___ ___ ___

45 Across   39 Across   64 Across

___ ___ ___ ___ ___ ___,   ___ ___ ___ ___

58 Across   3 Down   36 Across

___ ___ ___ ___ ___ ___ ___ ___ ___ ___.

49 Across   2 Down   28 Across

The Naval Treaty

BRIARBRAE, WOKING

MY DEAR WATSON:

Do you remember "Tadpole" Phelps from school? You may have heard that through my uncle, Lord Holdhurst, I had a post at the Foreign Office. A misfortune has blasted my career. I am just recovering from nine weeks of brain fever. Could you bring your friend Mr. Holmes to see me—though the police assure me nothing more can be done.

PERCY PHELPS

"The handwriting is a woman's," said Sherlock Holmes, after reading the letter Dr. Watson had brought him, "a woman of rare character. Certainly, we shall start at once for Woking."

Briarbrae was a large house standing in extensive grounds. Holmes and Watson were greeted in the drawing-room by a stout man, about thirty-five, with ruddy cheeks and merry eyes.

"I am Joseph Harrison," said he. "Percy is to marry my sister Annie; she came a few months ago, with myself as escort, to meet his people. We stayed on so that she could nurse him."

He led them to Percy's room on the same floor, where they found the pale young man on a sofa near a window open to the garden. With him was a striking, black-haired young woman, introduced as Miss Harrison. Phelps plunged into his story.

"Ten weeks ago, my uncle, in his capacity as foreign minister, called me into his office and gave me a grey roll of papers.

" 'This is a secret naval treaty between England and Italy of which rumors have already got into the press. The French or the Russians would pay a fortune for it now. A copy must be made; lock it in your desk, remain after hours to copy it. Relock the original and the copy; bring them to me tomorrow morning.' "

"Excuse me," said Holmes. "Were you and your uncle alone?"

"Yes," said Phelps, "in the center of the room, speaking in low voices; no one could have overheard. I did as my uncle asked. Another clerk in my room, Charles Gorot, stayed on a bit to finish up, so I went out to dine; he was gone when I returned. I hurried my work, for I knew that Joseph Harrison was in town and was to take the eleven o'clock train to Woking, and I wanted to catch it, too. But it was a long document; by nine o'clock I had copied only a third of it, and I was feeling drowsy. A porter remains all night in a room at the foot of the stairs, and makes coffee for those who work overtime. I rang the bell to summon him, but an elderly woman came up. She said she was the porter's wife, who did charing. I asked her for the coffee.

"I wrote two more pages, but my coffee had not yet come. I went down to find out why. A dimly lit passage leads from my room; it is the only exit from it. It ends in a curving staircase, with the porter's room at the bottom. Half-way down this staircase is a small landing, with another passage running into it at right angles. This second one leads down a small stair to a side door. Here is a rough chart of the place.

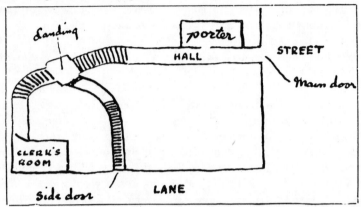

"I found the porter asleep, my coffee furiously aboil. I was about to wake him, when a bell over his head rang loudly. He woke, looked up at the still-shaking bell and then at me, astonished.

" 'Mr. Phelps! If you are here, who rang the bell in your room? The minis-ter said only you was supposed to stay late.'

"A cold hand seemed to close round my heart. I ran up the stair and along the passage. There was no one in the corridor, no one in the room—but the original treaty was gone! I knew at once the thief must have come up the stairs from the side door."

"Could he have been concealed in your room all the time, or in the dimly lit corridor?" asked Holmes.

"Impossible—there is no cover at all," said Phelps. "The porter had fol-lowed me upstairs, and we both rushed down the stairs to the side door. It was closed, but unlocked. We flung it open and rushed out. At the far corner we found a policeman.

" 'I have just been robbed! Has anyone passed this way?'

" 'Only a woman with a Paisley shawl—she seemed in a hurry.'

" 'That is only my wife,' cried the porter. 'Take my word, she has nothing to do with it. The thief may be on Whitehall!'

"With the policeman we both hurried there, only to find the street crowded with people. We returned to the office, and made a thorough search. The corridor showed no footmarks, though it had been raining all evening—the charwomen change to list slippers. The windows in the room are thirty feet from the ground, and were fastened on the inside. There's no fireplace—the thief could only have come in through the door. The bell-rope is just right of my desk. But why should a thief ring the bell?"

"It was most unusual," said Holmes. "What did you do next?"

"The only tangible fact was that the porter's wife—Mrs. Tangey—had hurried out of the place. The alarm had reached Scotland Yard; Mr. Forbes, the detective, came round at once, and we went to the porter's house. Mrs. Tangey had not returned, but her daughter showed us in. In ten minutes a knock came at the door. We heard the girl say, 'Mother, there are two men waiting for you,' and an instant later we heard Mrs. Tangey run into the kitchen. We ran after, but she had got there before us. She claimed she had thought we were bill collectors.

" 'We believe you have taken papers from the Foreign Office,' said Forbes. 'You must come to Scotland Yard to be searched.'

"First we searched the kitchen and its fireplace, in vain. The protesting woman was searched at Scotland Yard, in vain. For the first time, the horror of my situation came over me in full force. I must have become a raving maniac; the police put me on my train where, fortunately, they found my neighbor, Dr. Ferrier. They explained my plight, and left me in his care.

"It was clear to all when we arrived home that I was in for a long illness, so Joseph was bundled out of this cheery room, and it was turned into a sickroom. Here I raved for nine weeks. Dr. Ferrier treated me, Miss Harrison nursed me by day, and a hired nurse by night. My memory returned three days ago, and Mr. Forbes has been here. He said that after the Tangeys had been investigated, police suspicion rested on Charles Gorot because of his French name and his staying late. But as nothing was found to implicate him, the matter was dropped. You are my last hope, Mr. Holmes."

"I have but few questions to ask," said Holmes. "Did any of your friends or family visit you that day—I assume they all know their way about your office. Did you tell anyone of your task?"

"No one visited me, and I told no one of the treaty."

Holmes seemed to fall into a reverie, broken by Miss Harrison, who asked with a touch of asperity, "Do you have any clues?"

"The thief may have come in a cab if he left no footprints. We must return to London now. We shall come back tomorrow."

At Scotland Yard, Forbes, a small, foxy man, told Holmes and Watson that he was still having the Tangeys and Gorot shadowed.

At Downing Street, Lord Holdhurst received Holmes and Watson cordially. The tall, courtly lord stated that he had told no one the treaty was being copied. As yet the treaty had not been sold, he said, adding that it would soon be worthless to the thief—it would cease to be secret in a month.

A shaken Percy awaited Holmes and Watson the next day; Annie was with him in his room, nursing him after his latest trouble.

"Last night," said he, "was the first night I slept without a nurse in the room and without a sleeping draught. During the night I was aroused by a metallic click, and heard my window being opened. I flung open the shutters. A cloaked man, carrying a knife, was crouching at the window. Too weak to try to catch him, I rang the bell and shouted to rouse the house. Joseph and the groom found marks in the flower bed, but could not follow the trail across the grass, as the weather has been so dry."

Holmes paced about the room, excited by Phelps's experience. "Do you think you could walk round the house with me?" he asked.

"Yes, with Joseph's help," said Phelps.

"I should like a walk in the sunshine, too," said Annie.

"I must ask you to remain sitting exactly where you are," said Holmes.

Joseph having met them, the four men walked slowly about as Holmes carefully examined the ground, but the marks were blurred.

"The drawing-room windows are larger than Mr. Phelps's," he noted. "I should think the burglar would have chosen those."

"They are more visible from the road," suggested Harrison.

"Well," said Holmes, "let's go back and talk it over."

Percy Phelps, leaning on Joseph's arm, was walking slowly. Holmes strode quickly across the lawn, followed by Watson; they reached the bedroom window some time before the others came up.

"Miss Harrison," said Holmes tensely, "you must stay where you are all day —let nothing prevent you. It is of the utmost importance. When you go to bed lock the door of this room on the outside and keep the key. Percy will come to London with us. You will be serving him. Tell no one of my request!"

As Phelps and Harrison joined them, Holmes said, "It would be a very great help to me, Mr. Phelps, if you would come up to London with us."

Phelps agreed, but at the railway station Holmes calmly said that he himself would not be leaving Woking. He put Phelps in Watson's care, promising that he would see them the next morning. Watson and Phelps, talking it over, could find no satisfactory reason for this new development. Phelps spent a nervous day and night at Baker Street. Watson did his best to calm him.

A ravenous Holmes turned up the next morning, refusing to discuss anything until he had had his breakfast. Mrs. Hudson brought in three covers, and they all sat down at the table. Phelps, dejected, would not eat, but at Holmes's urging raised his cover. Across the center of his plate was lying a grey roll of papers.

"God bless you," cried Phelps. "You have saved my honour!"

"I tore it," said Holmes, "from the hands of Joseph Harrison."

"Joseph!" gasped Phelps. "Joseph a villain and a thief!"

"Several clues led me to Joseph," said Holmes. "In the first place, you were going to travel home with him that rainy night; it was likely enough that he should call for you in a cab. And there was real evidence that the person who stole the treaty had come for a sociable purpose rather than for thievery—the treaty was stolen on the spur of the moment when its value was recognized.

"Secondly, when I heard yesterday of the attempted intrusion into your room, in which Joseph had had the chance to conceal something before he was turned out, my suspicions turned to certainty for a good reason."

1) What real evidence did Holmes refer to in the first place? 2) What clue in the attempted intrusion confirmed his suspicions?

Across

1 "Oh, Johnny, I hardly ____ ye."
5 Bits of news
10 "I have ____ faithful to thee, Cynara! . . ."
14 Variable star
15 Bellini opera
16 King of Israel
17 Dill
18 Old German coin
19 "____, book and candle . . ."
20 O. Henry and family
22 Helium, argon, neon, etc.
24 Boor
25 In good health
26 Affix
29 Deceives
33 ____ culpa (my fault)
34 Auto style
36 Presidential candidate Stevenson
37 "____ is long, life short . . ."
38 Mystical
40 Geometric figure: Abbr.
41 Frown
44 Giver
46 Recent: Comb. form
47 Summaries
49 Marine worm
51 French ones
52 Hindu god of fire
53 "A dagger of the mind, ____ creation . . ."
56 Anterior
60 South African monetary unit
61 Wall Street unit
64 Contribute
65 Student's pony
66 City in ancient Egypt
67 King of Norway
68 Predicament
69 Clifford ____, U.S. playwright
70 Experienced

Down

1 Hilltop
2 Taboo, to a child
3 At all times
4 Jowl
5 Trespasser
6 Drink to
7 ____king (evil spirit)
8 Mrs., in Marseille
9 Noncoms
10 Snow vehicle for racing
11 Scottish uncles
12 Mystery writer Gardner
13 Silent screen star Asther
21 Eternities
23 ____ breve (musical sign)
25 ____ a walk (finish in front easily)
26 Accumulate
27 Henry ____ (Hotspur)
28 ____ the back (compliment)
29 Spanish hands
30 Solitary
31 Close to: Ger.
32 Fodder pits
35 Dandies
39 U.S. legislature
42 ____ gentleman (parvenu)
43 Nursing personnel: Abbr.
45 Nevadan city
48 Looks after
50 ____ the Nibelung
52 Evil jinni
53 Prefix for bishop or duke
54 Card game
55 Source of blue dye
57 Roofing piece
58 Grandparental
59 Departed
62 Owned
63 One: Scot.

Puzzle XIII: *The Naval Treaty*

Solution and epilogue on page 152

1) __ __ __ __   __ __   __ __ __ __ __ __ __ __   ,   __ __ __ __ __ __.
   50 Down   20 Across   19 Across

2) __ __ __ __ __ - __ __   __ __ __ __ __ __ __ __ __   __ __ __ __
   42 Down   5 Down   1 Across

__ __ __ __ __ __   __ __ __ __ __   __ __ __ __ __ __.
27 Down   62 Down   10 Across   59 Down   30 Down

Although Sherlock Holmes had foiled the machinations of many villains and seemed to be invulnerable, he could not escape Conan Doyle's decision in 1893 to do away with the world's first and "only unofficial consulting detective." Doyle was enamored of the medieval history of England, and wanted to devote his time to writing historical romances. So, to the anguish of Sherlock Holmes fans around the globe, he sent Holmes and archvillain Professor Moriarty hurtling to death over the Reichenbach Falls in "The Final Problem." The story, set in 1891, was told by Watson who assumed, as did the rest of the world, that Holmes and Moriarty, locked in a death struggle, had reeled into the roaring waters and had vanished forever.

But public sentiment would not allow Holmes to die. Pressure came from both the public and the publishers, and in 1901 *The Hound of the Baskervilles* appeared in serial form. Holmes had not been entirely resurrected, however, for the story was set in 1889, before his death.

The great detective comes to full life again in the following story, "The Adventure of the Empty House," which was published in 1903, ten years after Doyle had made away with him. This story takes place in 1894, leaving a fictional gap of only three years, which Doyle neatly bridges in the course of the story.

Holmes is back to stay for many more adventures, as brilliant, as resourceful, and as daring as ever.

Ruth Lake Tepper

The Adventure of the Empty House

D r. Watson suffered two grievous losses between the years 1891 and 1894. His beloved wife, Mary, and his good friend, Sherlock Holmes, had died, leaving him quite alone, missing them sorely. He still maintained his interest in crime, and sadly noted that the cause of justice, too, had been dealt a severe blow by Holmes's death. He was keenly aware of this as he stood, one day in the spring of '94, among a throng of people looking up at a particular window in Park Lane, behind which the Honorable Ronald Adair had been murdered. The police investigation and the inquest had proved only that the case was insoluble.

The second son of the Earl of Maynooth, Adair had come to London with his mother who was to undergo an operation, and they had taken the house in Park Lane. The young man had no known enemies and no particular vices. He had a fondness for cards, and belonged to several clubs. Though his fortune was large, he was a cautious player for low stakes, and usually won. On the night of his death he had played at the Bagatelle. At the inquest, the evidence of those who had played with him—Mr. Murray, Sir John Hardy, and Colonel Sebastian Moran—showed that Adair had lost five pounds. However, in partnership with Colonel Moran, he had recently won four hundred pounds in a sitting.

When Adair came home on the fatal night, his mother was out. The servant deposed that she had heard him enter the front room on the second floor, where earlier she had lit a fire, and as it smoked, had opened the window. She had heard no further sound from the room. Adair's mother, returning home and wishing to say good night, had knocked at her son's door. Getting no reply and finding the door locked on the inside, Lady Maynooth had had the door forced. Adair was found lying near a table, his head mutilated by an expanding revolver bullet. No weapon was found in the room. On the table, thirty pounds in banknotes and coins were arranged in piles of varying amounts, near a sheet of paper with figures on it and the names of club friends opposite them—apparently a list of losses and winnings.

There seemed no reason for Adair to have locked the door on the inside, nor could the murderer have done so and then escaped by the window, for there was a drop of twenty feet to a garden below, which was found undisturbed. No one could have climbed up to the window without leaving traces. It was difficult to suppose that someone had fired through the window; he would have been a remarkable shot indeed to have made that wound with a revolver. No one had heard a shot; there was no known motive, no robbery.

Such was the Park Lane Mystery. Everyone had a theory, including some vocal members of the throng in front of Adair's house. They seemed absurd to Watson. He withdrew in some disgust, striking against a deformed old man and knocking down several books the man was carrying. Helping to pick

87

them up, Watson noticed their obscure subjects and guessed the fellow to be a bibliophile or a bookseller. He had not been at home five minutes, when the old man, who had apparently followed him, came calling.

"I have brought you some books," he croaked, "bargains! With five volumes you could fill that gap on the second shelf."

Watson moved his head to look at the cabinet behind him. He turned again, to find Sherlock Holmes standing before him, smiling. For the first time in his life, Watson fainted. When he came to, Holmes was bending over him with a glass of brandy.

"My dear Watson," said Holmes, "a thousand apologies!"

"Holmes!" cried Watson. "Is it really you? Tell me how you came alive out of that dreadful chasm!"

"If I may ask your cooperation," said Holmes, "we have a dangerous night's work ahead. I will explain everything later."

"I should prefer to hear it now," said Watson.

"Well, then," said Holmes, "I had no difficulty in getting out of the chasm, because I was never in it. I know baritsu—Japanese wrestling—and I slid through Moriarty's grip. He lost his balance, and over he went. It struck me what a lucky chance Fate had handed me. I knew that three members of Moriarty's gang would not rest until they had got me. But if all the world were convinced that I was dead, they would take liberties, and sooner or later I could get them. Then it would be time for me to come alive. My apologies, Watson, but would you have written so convincingly of my end had you not believed it?

"I did not want to leave any tracks on the path, so I decided to climb up the sheer cliff. I reached a ledge and was resting, when a huge rock boomed past me. I looked up and saw a man's head against the darkening sky—it was a confederate of Moriarty! I scrambled down, torn and bleeding, and did ten miles over the mountains in the dark. Now the Moriarty gang would know that I lived, but not what had become of me. For three years I traveled round the world, disguised as Sigerson, a Norwegian. You may have read of his remarkable explorations, never knowing that they were your friend's. I had one confidant—my brother Mycroft.

"Learning that only one of my enemies was left in London, I was preparing to return when I read of the Park Lane Mystery, and hastened back. I returned today in my own person to Baker Street, threw Mrs. Hudson into hysterics, and found that Mycroft had preserved my rooms intact. Now we have work ahead, Watson!"

It was like old times when Holmes and Watson, his revolver in his pocket, set out at half-past nine, taking a tortuous route to their destination—the back of an empty house. They entered, then made their way in the dark to a large room, heavily shadowed in the corners, but faintly lit in the center by the lights of the street beyond. The window was thick with dust.

"Surely that is Baker Street," whispered Watson, staring out.

"We are directly opposite our old quarters," said Holmes. "Draw nearer to the window, and look up at the sitting room."

Watson gave a cry of amazement. The blind was down, and on it was the silhouette of a man seated in a chair—a perfect reproduction of Sherlock Holmes! Holmes explained that it was a wax bust which Mrs. Hudson would move slightly every quarter-hour.

"My rooms were being watched by Moriarty's gang; I recognized their sentinel. They believed that I should come back some day. Their new leader, the dangerous rock-thrower of the Reichenbach Falls, is after me tonight—not knowing that we are after *him*."

Holmes and Watson waited silently in the darkness. At midnight Holmes suddenly became tense, and pulled Watson into the blackest corner of the room. A man crept in and stole over to the window, raising it a foot. As he sank to the level of the opening the streetlight revealed him to be elderly, with a bald forehead and a huge moustache. He carried an oddly shaped gun, the barrel of which he rested on the window ledge. As he peered through the sights, his finger tightened on the trigger. There was a strange whizz and a tinkle of broken glass. At that instant Holmes sprang at him, hurling him to the floor. He was up in a moment, and seized Holmes by the throat. Watson quickly hit him on the head with the butt of his revolver, and he dropped to the floor. Holmes blew a shrill call on a whistle that brought Inspector Lestrade and two policemen running into the house.

"It's good to have you back, Mr. Holmes," said Lestrade.

Candles were lit, and Holmes and Watson were able to have a good look at their prisoner, whose eyes were fixed on Holmes's face with an expression that blended hatred with amazement.

"You fiend," he kept muttering. "You clever, clever fiend!"

"This, gentlemen," said Holmes, "is Colonel Sebastian Moran, once of her Majesty's Indian Army, and the best of heavy game shots. Colonel, you surprised me. I had imagined you operating from the street, where Lestrade and his men were waiting for you."

Holmes picked up the powerful air-gun and examined it.

"Admirable," said he, "and noiseless. I knew the man who constructed it for the late Professor Moriarty. For years I have been aware of its existence. This is the man and the gun, Lestrade, that killed Ronald Adair through his open window."

Walking across to 221B, Holmes remarked to Watson that on reading of Adair's murder he had at once connected Moran with it.

"But what was his motive for murdering Adair?" asked Watson.

"Ah, that is in the realm of conjecture, and your hypothesis may be as good as mine. I have formed one that may pass."

Holmes's theory: Adair had discovered that Moran had cheated at cards; he threatened to expose him unless Moran did as he asked. 1) What did Adair want Colonel Moran to do? 2) Why did the Colonel decide to kill Adair rather than to do as he asked?

Across

1 Wyatt _____, lawman
5 Breed of dog
9 "Let me _____ the fool."
13 Wrath
14 Troublemaker in Norse mythology
15 Hawaiian tree
16 Permission
17 "Pure _____ . . ."
19 Experiments with
21 Clamor
22 "Moonlight," and others
23 Dreadful
24 _____ down (disappoint)
25 Incantations
28 "_____ seek to tell thy love . . ."
31 Latin American dance
32 Law degree
34 Mimicked
35 In the _____ (likely)

36 Cudgel
37 Bridle part
38 Eel
39 Mislays
40 Rank below brigadier general
42 Border
43 Lawyers: Abbr.
44 Bows: Eng. Dial.
48 Adhesive
50 Put right
51 Untruthful
53 Dignified: Fr.
54 Poker stake
55 Hindu good spirit
56 Czech statesman
57 "Elaine, the lily _____ of Astolat."
58 Flower parts: Abbr.
59 Belgian river

Down

1 January in Jerez
2 "Come _____ another day."
3 Made known
4 _____ John, legendary medieval king
5 Santa _____
6 Innkeeper
7 Russian river
8 Profits
9 Burro's basket
10 Hauls
11 Away from the wind
12 Actor Brynner
13 Elevations: Abbr.
18 Main heart artery
20 Cereal grain
23 "Yankee Doodle _____ . . ."
25 Fable conclusion
26 Word in a Shakespeare title
27 Swing around
28 Collar

29 *The Odyssey*, for example
30 Refuse consent to
31 Worries
33 Radio industry initials
35 Vies
36 Farces
38 Saying
39 _____ one's wits (cheated)
41 Flogged
42 Gypsy man
44 Chemical prefixes
45 Actress Hasso
46 To have: Sp.
47 Poems by Pindar
48 Kind of cloth
49 Italian wine district
50 Invitation initials
51 Weir
52 Shoe width

Puzzle XIV:
The Adventure of the Empty House

Solution and epilogue on page 153

1) __ __ __ __ __ __ __ __ __ ; __ __ __ __ __ __ __ __ __ __
  16 Across   36 Across   28 Across   9 Across

__ __ __ __ __ __ __ __ __ __ __ 2) __ __ __ __ __ __
35 Across   2 Down   40 Across

__ __ __ __ __ __ __ __ __ __ __ __ __ __ __ __
39 Down   51 Across

__ __ __ __ __ __ __ __.
8 Down

Sherlock in Disguise

*P*Sherlock Holmes obviously enjoyed his fantastic ability to assume the guises of a wide range of characters, but his talent was used for a serious purpose—to investigate aspects and areas of his cases which otherwise would have been dangerous or impossible to explore.

Holmes's disguises were no mere dressing up or playacting, although he was a master of makeup and a consummate actor. He had to bring to each character an intimate acquaintance of the character's milieu, the tricks of his trade, his speech and general behavior, for Holmes's very life often depended on having verisimilitude accepted as reality. Imagine, then, the knowledge of the world and of human nature that lay behind the disguises.

It was, of course, Conan Doyle, Holmes's creator, who was the font. Doyle was an omnivorous reader, a constant traveler, interested and involved in countless activities: the theater, music, medicine, law, the sciences; aside from being a born storyteller and a writer of staggering productivity, he was in the course of his life a whaler, medical practitioner, inventor, sportsman, reformer, politician, war correspondent, battler for causes, lecturer, historian, and—an amateur detective.

So important was disguise to Holmes's investigations that he kept at least five small refuges in different parts of London, presumably well stocked with costumes, wigs, cosmetics, and other paraphernalia necessary to his transformations, where he could quickly change from himself to whomever the occasion called for. And so rich were his characterizations that even his best friend, Watson, could not pierce the masquerades. Watson (or Doyle) has given us some marvelous descriptions of Sherlock Holmes in disguise.

● In *The Sign of Four*: "A heavy step was heard ascending the stair, with a great wheezing and rattling as from a man who was sorely put to it for breath. Once or twice he stopped, as though the climb were too much for him, but at last he made his way to our door and entered. His appearance corresponded to the sounds which we had heard. He was an aged man, clad in seafaring garb, with an old pea-jacket buttoned up to his throat. His back was bowed, his knees were shaky, and his breathing was painfully asthmatic. As he leaned upon a thick cudgel his shoulders heaved in the effort to draw the air into his lungs. He had a coloured scarf round his chin, and I could see little of his face save a pair of keen dark eyes, overhung by bushy white brows and long gray side-whiskers. Altogether he gave me the impression of a respectable master mariner who had fallen into years and poverty."

The "groom" in "A Scandal in Bohemia."

● In "A Scandal in Bohemia": "He disappeared into his bedroom and returned in a few minutes in the character of an amiable and simple-minded Nonconformist clergyman. His broad black hat, his baggy trousers, his white tie, his sympathetic smile, and general look of peering and benevolent curiosity were such as Mr. John Hare alone could have equalled. It was not merely that Holmes changed his costume. His expression, his manner, his very soul seemed to vary with every fresh part that he assumed. The stage lost a fine actor, even as science lost an acute reasoner, when he became a specialist in crime."

● In "The Final Problem": "The station clock marked only seven minutes from the time when we were due to start. In vain I searched among the groups of travellers and leave-takers for the lithe figure of my friend. There was no sign of him. I spent a few minutes in assisting a venerable Italian priest, who was endeavouring to make a porter understand, in his broken English, that his luggage was to be booked through to Paris. Then, having taken another look round, I returned to my carriage, where I found that the porter, in spite of the ticket, had given me my decrepit Italian friend as a travelling companion. It was useless for me to explain to him that his presence was an intrusion, for my Italian was even more limited than his English. . . . I turned in uncontrollable astonishment. The aged ecclesiastic had turned his face towards me. For an instant the wrinkles were smoothed away, the nose drew away from the chin, the lower lip ceased to protrude and the mouth to mumble, the dull eyes regained their fire, the drooping figure expanded. The next, the whole frame collapsed again, and Holmes had gone as quickly as he had come."

The roles go on and on. In The "Adventure of the Empty House," Holmes was an elderly, deformed bookseller, with a curved back and white sidewhiskers, dressed in a seedy frock coat. His voice croaked. In "The Adventure of Charles Augustus Milverton," he was a rakish young plumber, with a goatee beard, a swagger, and a rising business, who had gotten himself engaged to Milverton's housemaid. When Watson protested on the girl's behalf, Holmes explained, " '. . . I rejoice to say that I have a hated rival, who will certainly cut me out the instant that my back is turned.' "

The "Italian priest" in "The Final Problem."

The Adventure of the Norwood Builder

It was a summer day of '94, and Watson, at Sherlock Holmes's request, was again sharing their old quarters at Baker Street. They had just breakfasted, when a frantic, wild-eyed young man burst into the room. He was dishevelled, but handsome and well dressed.

"I am the unhappy John McFarlane," he cried. "I am being followed, Mr. Holmes! If they come to arrest me, make them give me time to tell the truth. Here is the terrible newspaper story!"

Taking the paper from the shaken young man, Watson read aloud:

> *Mr. Jonas Oldacre, wealthy builder at Lower Norwood, is believed to have been slain last night at his home. The retired fifty-two-year-old bachelor maintained a small timber-yard back of his house; about midnight one of the stacks was entirely consumed by fire. Mr. Oldacre could not be found, and a search of his bedroom on the ground floor revealed signs of a struggle. A safe in the room was open, papers were strewn about, and traces of blood were found in the room and on an oaken walking stick. The stick was identified as belonging to Mr. John McFarlane, a London solicitor who had visited Mr. Oldacre late last night. French windows in the bedroom were open, and a bulky object had been dragged from there to the woodpile. Small charred remains have been found in the ashes. A warrant has been issued for the arrest of Mr. McFarlane. Inspector Lestrade of Scotland Yard is conducting the criminal investigation.*

No sooner had Watson read the paragraph than Lestrade appeared in the doorway to arrest McFarlane for Oldacre's murder. Granting Holmes's request, he allowed McFarlane half an hour.

"Years ago my parents knew Mr. Oldacre," said McFarlane. "I first met him yesterday when he came to my office to have his will made, a strange ferretlike man. I was astonished to find I was to be his heir. I stammered out my thanks, the will was drawn, signed, witnessed. Here it is. He begged me to come to his house last night to see important papers, and to say nothing to my parents—he wished to surprise them. I sent a telegram home to Blackheath, telling my parents I would be late. I arrived at Norwood nine o'clock, and was announced by Mr. Oldacre's housekeeper. He led me to his bedroom, and took from his safe a mass of leases and deeds. It was almost twelve when we finished going over them. He showed me out through his French window; I left him with the safe open, and the papers, some of which I helped make into packets and seal with wax, on the table. I could not find my walking stick. It was too late to return home, so I spent the night at an inn, and knew nothing of this horrible affair until I read about it on the train this morning."

After Lestrade left with McFarlane, Holmes remarked to Watson, "Would an heir choose the very night after the will has been made to kill his benefactor? I am going to Blackheath for some light on this curious will, so suddenly made. I hope to help the unfortunate youngster who has sought my help."

But Holmes returned that evening in a state of great disappointment. "What I learned at Blackheath only strengthens the police case. Oldacre was a bitter, rejected suitor of Mrs. McFarlane, who described him as cruel and malignant. Her son may have heard her speak this way, and learned to hate him. I then went to Norwood. Oldacre's trouser buttons have been found in the ashes; his housekeeper identified them. She is a sly one; I think she knows more than she is telling. I found only one gleam of hope: the leases and deeds are of small value, and Oldacre's bankbook has a low balance—he made out large checks this past year to a Mr. Cornelius. It must be looked into."

The next morning a telegram from Lestrade was delivered to Holmes. "Listen to this, Watson: 'Important fresh evidence. McFarlane's guilt established. Advise you to abandon case.' "

When Holmes and Watson arrived at Norwood to examine the fresh evidence, Lestrade led them to a dark hall in the house.

"This is where McFarlane got his hat after the crime was done," said Lestrade. "Look at this." He lit a match; its light exposed a bloody thumbprint on the whitewashed wall. "It matches our wax impression of McFarlane's thumb. It is final."

"Yes, final," said Holmes, grinning. "Who discovered it?"

"The housekeeper found it. If you have anything further to say, I shall be in the sitting room writing my report."

Holmes, in great good humor, set about with Watson to examine the outside and the inside of the house minutely.

"I *know* that mark was not there when I examined the hall yesterday. Now *I* have some new evidence for friend Lestrade."

Telling Lestrade he had found an important witness, Holmes asked the angry inspector to have his men bring straw and buckets of water to the top floor. He then directed them to place the straw near the wall at the end of the broad corridor.

"Put a match to the straw," said Holmes, "and cry 'Fire!' "

The shout had hardly died away, when a door flew open out of what had appeared to be the solid wall at the corridor's end, and a little wizened man darted out like a rabbit from its burrow.

"Watson, a bucket of water on the straw. Lestrade, let me present Mr. Jonas Oldacre. He had conceived a perfect plan, but gilded the lily by putting the thumbprint on the wall last night."

"But how?" asked Lestrade.

Holmes had deduced how Oldacre had managed to put McFarlane's thumbprint, in blood, on the wall. 1) On what had the print originally been made? 2) How did Oldacre transfer it to the wall?

Across

1 Feeler
5 Nigerian natives
9 _____ Missouri (skeptical)
13 Craze
14 Salamander
15 Hercules's captive
16 Caper
17 Zola novel
18 City in California
19 By: Ger.
20 Long-tailed monkeys
22 "I only _____ that I have but one life . . ."
24 Icy rain
26 Impel
27 Airy swiftness
30 Sorrow
34 Digestive enzyme
35 Plainclothesmen: Slang
37 Engineering degree
38 Letter
39 Tree knot

41 Favorite
42 _____ Baba
43 "Set me as a _____ upon thine heart . . ."
44 Go on _____ (carouse)
47 Middle, in law
49 Payers
51 Toward the mouth
53 Pile up
54 Sawbuck
57 Organization: Abbr.
58 Short time, for short
61 Melville novel
62 Grain breads
64 Deer: It.
66 Leave out
67 Appraise
68 Kind of bank
69 Cabbage
70 Hews
71 Desires

Down

1 Window glass
2 Use of germicides
3 Weeks in a year: Rom. num.
4 Boats plying regular route
5 Natural
6 Miss Lillie, and others
7 _____ up (admit)
8 Beatle Ringo
9 New York's _____ Lakes
10 Bellow
11 Wine jug
12 Kind of pie
13 Fairy queen
21 Back out
23 Makings of an omelet
25 Meadow
26 Employer
27 Old lancet
28 Strong cotton thread
29 "How weary, _____, flat and unprofitable . . ."

31 Dental mold
32 Moslem ruler
33 Galas
36 Prospector's stakes
40 Ointment
43 Withered
45 Understudy
46 Components: Abbr.
48 Take _____ of (disregard)
50 "Your huddled _____ yearning to be free . . ."
52 Macaw
54 _____ in hand (disciplined)
55 Madame Bovary
56 Wool shreds
57 Prefix for room or date
59 Adam's grandson
60 Food fish
63 Paraffin
65 *Cakes and* _____

Puzzle XV:
The Adventure of the Norwood Builder

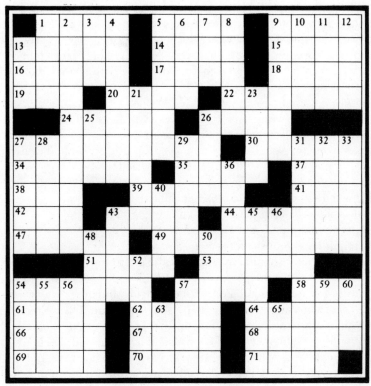

Solution and epilogue on page 154

1) __ __ __ __ __ __ __'__ __ __ __ __ __ __ __ __.
     4 Down   63 Down   43 Across

2) __ __ __ __ __
     54 Down

__ __ __ __   __ __ __ __ __ __ __ __ __ __ __   __ __ __ __ __   __ __ __ __ __,

63 Down   31 Down   9 Across   43 Across

__ __ __ __ __   __ __ __ __ __   __ __ __ __   __ __ __ __ __ __ __.

68 Across   9 Across   7 Down   9 Down

The Adventure of Black Peter

During the first week of July '95, Holmes was often absent without explanation from Baker Street, and several rough-looking men called asking for Captain Basil. Watson understood, then, that Holmes was working somewhere in one of his many disguises, and got his first inkling of the case when Holmes came in one day carrying a huge spear under his arm.

"Had you looked in back of Allardyce's butcher shop," said Holmes, "you would have seen me trying to transfix a dead pig with a single blow of this spear. I was not strong enough."

"But why were you doing this?" asked Watson.

"It may bear on the mystery of Woodman's Lee. Ah, Hopkins, come in, I got your wire. I have already read about your case."

Stanley Hopkins, an alert, young police inspector who Holmes had taken under his wing, entered with an air of deep dejection.

"I can see you have made no progress," said Holmes. "What about that tobacco pouch that was found at the scene of the crime?"

"It was the man's own pouch, sir. His initials were inside."

"But he had no pipe," said Holmes.

"He might have kept the tobacco for his friends."

"No doubt, but I should have made it the starting point of the investigation. Please sketch the matter for Dr. Watson."

"The dead man, Captain Peter Carey," said Hopkins, "was a seal and whale fisher, who commanded the sealer *Sea Unicorn*, until he retired in 1884. He bought a small place called Woodman's Lee in Sussex, where he lived with his wife and daughter until he was killed last Wednesday. He was a violent, cruel man, and a drunkard, who was known to flog his family. In the trade he was called Black Peter, not only because of his huge beard, but also for his terrible rages. He had built, some yards from his house, a one-room cabin, which he fitted out like a captain's room, with a bunk, a sea-chest, logbooks, and a picture of the *Sea Unicorn*. Here he slept every night; he kept the key in his pocket, and no one was allowed to enter. There are small windows on two sides of the cabin, which were curtained and never opened. The window facing the high road gave us a bit of evidence.

"A stonemason named Slater, walking on the road at one o'clock in the morning—two days before the murder—saw a light burning in the cabin, and the shadow of a man's head clearly visible on the blind. It was that of a man with a short beard, very different from the captain's. About two o'clock on Wednesday morning, Carey's daughter heard a fearful yell from the cabin, but it was usual for him to shout when he was drunk, so no notice was taken. It was midday before anyone dared to look through the open door. In an hour, I was on the spot, and had taken over the case. My nerves are fairly steady, but I shook when I walked inside. Right through Carey's broad breast a steel harpoon had been driven, and had sunk deep into the wall behind him.

"The harpoon had been snatched from a rack on the wall; on its shaft was engraved, 'SS *Sea Unicorn* Dundee.' Though the crime was committed at two in the morning, Peter Carey was fully dressed, suggesting that he had had an appointment with the murderer. There were a bottle of rum and two dirty glasses on the table, and also that sealskin pouch with 'P. C.' inside the flap; it contained ship's tobacco. Carey's sheathed knife, identified by his wife, lay at his feet. But *this* was not at the inquest—"

Hopkins drew a small, worn notebook from his pocket. On the first page were written the initials "J. H. N." and the date "1883." On the second page was printed "Canadian Pacific Railway," and then came several sheets of numbers. Another heading was "Argentina," and another "San Paulo," each with figures.

"I believe," said he, "that the initials 'J. H. N.' are those of the second person who was present, and this listing of valuable securities gives us a possible motive. But it will be weeks before inquiries into the shares are completed. I picked the book off the floor; the bloodstain on its cover was on the side next the boards, which proves that the book was dropped after the crime was committed. None of the securities was found among the property of the dead man."

"Have you any reason to suspect robbery?" asked Holmes.

"No, sir. Nothing seems to have been touched."

"I shall come out and have a look," said Holmes, as Hopkins gave a cry of joy. "I should be glad of your company, Watson."

The cabin turned out to be a simple dwelling, with one window beside the door and one on the farther side. Hopkins put the key in the lock, and paused with a look of surprise.

"Someone has been tampering with it," he said.

The woodwork was cut, and scratches showed white through the paint. Holmes had been examining the window.

"Someone has tried to force this also. He failed to make his way in. I think fortune is very kind to us. He will probably try again tonight with a better tool. We must welcome him."

Holmes next examined the inside of the cabin carefully.

"Something has been taken from this shelf, Hopkins! There's less dust in this corner than elsewhere. It may be a box."

At eleven o'clock the three men formed their ambuscade in the bushes round the far window. Two o'clock had chimed when a stealthy step was heard. This time the man succeeded in entering. He lit a candle, and through the curtain they could see that the visitor was young, well dressed, frail and thin. He picked up a logbook and rapidly turned the pages. Finding what he sought, with an angry gesture he closed the book, and replaced it. He was about to put out the light, when Hopkins' hand was on his collar.

"'Someone has been tampering with it,' he said."

"You must be detectives," said the shivering young man. "I assure you I am innocent of the death of Peter Carey. Please let me explain." He tried to compose himself. "My name is John Hopley Neligan. Did you ever hear of Dawson and Neligan?"

"You mean the bankers who failed for a million," said Holmes, "and ruined half the county of Cornwall. Neligan disappeared."

"Exactly. It was twelve years ago. Neligan was my father, and the one really concerned; Dawson had retired. It has been said that my father stole all the securities and fled—it is not true! It was his belief that if he were given time to realize them, all would be well and every creditor paid in full. He started in his little yacht for Norway just before the warrant was issued for his arrest. He left my mother and me a list of the securities he was taking. Both the yacht and he vanished utterly; we assumed they were at the bottom of the sea. You can imagine our amazement when a friend discovered some of the securities on the London market. After months of tracing them, I discovered that the original seller had been Captain Peter Carey. I found that the *Sea Unicorn* and my father's ship, blown by a gale, could have crossed routes in August, 1883. If I could prove from Peter Carey that my father had not sold the securities, I might clear his name. I came to Sussex with the intention of seeing Carey, but he had just been murdered. I tried to get a look at the logbook last night, but couldn't get in. Tonight I succeeded, but the pages for August, 1883, have been torn from the book."

"If you have not been here before last night," cried Hopkins, holding up the damning notebook, "how do you account for that?"

Neligan trembled. "Where did you get it?" he groaned.

"That is enough," said Hopkins sternly. "Whatever else you have to say, you must say in court. Mr. Holmes, I am very much obliged and grateful, though I could have solved the case myself."

The next morning Holmes observed to Watson, "I am disappointed in Stanley Hopkins. One should always look for a possible alternative. It is the first rule of criminal investigation. I myself have been pursuing such an alternative."

The morning mail brought Holmes good news. "The alternative develops, Watson. My experiment with the spear showed me a way. Neligan cannot possibly be the murderer. But I may have found a way to locate the criminal. Just write a couple of wires for me: 'Sumner, Shipping Agent, Ratcliff Highway. Send three men on, to arrive ten tomorrow morning—Basil.' That's my name in those parts. The other is: 'Inspector Stanley Hopkins, 46 Lord Street, Brixton. Come breakfast nine-thirty tomorrow morning. Important—Sherlock Holmes.' This infernal case has haunted me for several days. Tomorrow, I trust, we shall hear the last of it."

1) Why was Holmes sure that Neligan was not the murderer? 2) Who were the three men Holmes had wired for? 3) Which one, in particular, was he looking for? Could you guess from the clues?

Across

1 Sweet potato
4 Arabian robes
8 Hautboy
12 Solo
14 Spaghetti, for example
16 "_____ the halls of Montezuma . . ."
17 Some of the crew of the *Pequod*
19 Ended: Slang
20 Pan and Piper
21 Best
23 Adherent
24 "Liberty and _____, now and forever . . ."
25 French count
28 Raging
29 _____-fi
32 Jacob's twin brother
33 Here: Fr.
34 Depth charge: Slang
36 Sour
37 More agreeable
39 Formerly, formerly
40 Saturday, in Paris
42 "_____ if by land . . ."
43 "_____ this Ring . . ."
44 Vocalized pauses
45 Roman highways
47 Small error
48 _____ Boru, Irish king
49 Long-leaved lettuce
50 _____ a statue (motionless)
53 _____ on (hired)
56 Actress Turner
57 Tots
60 Heroic
61 Caravansary
62 "_____, you old gypsy man . . ."
63 Feeble
64 Hindu music
65 Prefix for meter or gram

Down

1 Derisive shout
2 Not care _____
3 Bog
4 Larboard
5 Outlaws
6 Peer Gynt's mother
7 _____ point (forte)
8 ". . . rode madly _____ all directions."
9 Cup edge
10 Mrs. Charlie Chaplin
11 Actor Jannings
13 Kind of test
15 Inhale: It.
18 Bacteriologist's wire loop
22 Playthings
24 "The lion and the _____ . . ."
25 Discontinue
26 Academy Award
27 Disables
28 Sicilian seaport
29 Temporary exchange medium
30 Molds
31 "_____ Good Old Summertime"
33 First letters
35 "_____ of an age but for all time."
38 Naval officer: Abbr.
41 Tingle: Scot. Dial.
46 Less difficult
47 Theater box
48 Kind of magic
49 Eyelashes
50 Great deal
51 It can be magnetic
52 Porpoise genus
53 Hart
54 English playwright Bagnold
55 Half: Prefix
58 _____-la-la
59 Coral or Red

Puzzle XVI:
The Adventure of Black Peter

Solution and epilogue on page 155

1) __ __ __ __ __ __ __ __ __ __ __ __ __ __ .

   35 Down   7 Down

2) __ __ __ __ __ __ __ __ __ __ __ __ .   3) __ __ __ __ __ __ __ __

   17 Across   42 Across   16 Across

__ __ __ __ __ __ __ __ __ __ __ __ __ __ __ __ __ __ __

59 Down   24 Down   43 Across   48 Down

__ __ __ __ __ , __ __ __ __ __ __ __ __ __ __ .

20 Across   33 Down

The Adventure of the Six Napoleons

"There's a madman in London," said Inspector Lestrade, visiting one evening with Sherlock Holmes and Watson, "who so hates Napoleon that he even commits burglaries to destroy images of him. Four days ago, while the clerk at Morse Hudson's statue shop was in the rear, the madman came in, smashed a plaster bust of Napoleon and vanished. Dr. Barnicot, the well-known physician, had recently purchased two of the busts from Hudson's, one for his home, and one for his surgery two miles away. Last night the madman stole the one from his home and dashed it against the garden wall; this morning the other was found strewn over the surgery."

"There is method to the man's madness," remarked Holmes. "He took the bust outside Dr. Barnicot's home, so as not to rouse the family. The other two were broken where they stood. Let me hear of any fresh developments."

Holmes had not long to wait—the next morning a telegram from Lestrade asked him to come to 131 Pitt Street. Holmes and Watson found him at the home of Horace Harker, a journalist.

"About four months ago," said Harker, "I bought a bust of Napoleon from Harding Brothers. Last night, working late in my den, I heard a horrible yell. I seized a poker and went down to my sitting room. The window was open, the bust gone. On my doorstep was a dead man, with his throat slit."

"There's nothing to show who he was," said Lestrade. "A clasp knife was found near him, and in his pocket was this snapshot." It showed an alert man with thick eyebrows and a heavy jaw.

"And what became of the bust?" asked Holmes.

"It was just found near an empty house a hundred yards away."

Holmes and Watson accompanied Lestrade to the empty house, where they found the bust scattered in shards on the lawn.

"This trifling plaster bust was worth more to our strange criminal than a human life," said Holmes. "Notice, it was not broken in the house or by the house, but near this streetlamp."

"By Jove!" said Lestrade, "Dr. Barnicot's was broken near a streetlamp, too. But now—we must identify the dead man."

"We must each go our own way," said Holmes. "Tell Mr. Harker I believe the murderer is a homicidal lunatic with Napoleonic delusions."

"You don't seriously believe that!" exclaimed Lestrade.

"Just tell him," said Holmes, smiling. "May I keep this snapshot? If convenient, please meet us at Baker Street at six."

At Morse Hudson's, Holmes and Watson learned that the peppery dealer had bought only three busts of Napoleon from Gelder & Co.'s sculpture works in Stepney. Holmes showed him the snapshot.

"Why, it's Beppo. Italian piecework man, useful in the shop. Could carve a bit. Left me last week, don't know where he is."

The manager at Gelder & Co. told Holmes that the three busts sent to

Morse Hudson a year or so ago had been half of a batch of six; the other three were sent to Harding Brothers. Italians usually made the plaster casts, which were set in a passage to dry, then stored. The photograph angered him.

"Ah, the rascal!" he cried. "He worked here, and the only time we had the police here was because of him. He knifed another Italian, and served a year. He got out a month ago. We employ his cousin; he can tell you where he is."

"No!" cried Holmes. "Not a word to the cousin, I beg you."

On the way to Harding Brothers, Holmes bought a newspaper. "This is fine, Watson," said he. "Mr. Horace Harker has blamed it all on lunacy, making our criminal feel quite secure."

The founder of Harding Brothers was a crisp man who quickly named the buyers of his three busts of Napoleon: Horace Harker, Mr. Josiah Brown, of Laburnum Villa, Chiswick, and Mr. Sandeford, of Reading. Yes, he had Italians on his staff; no, no watch was kept on the sales book. He did not know the man in the snapshot.

When Holmes and Watson returned home to Baker Street at six, they found Lestrade waiting for them impatiently.

"I have identified the dead man, and found a cause for the crime!" he cried. "His name is Pietro Venucci; he was a member of the Mafia, a secret political society. The fellow in the photograph is probably an Italian, too, and a member of the same group, who broke the rules. Pietro is given his photograph; he dogs the fellow, waits for him outside Harker's house, and is killed in the scuffle. How is that, Mr. Sherlock Holmes?"

"Excellent," said Holmes, "but what about the busts?"

"The busts!" cried Lestrade. "Can't you get them out of your head? We are going to the Italian Quarter to find the murderer."

"I suggest you come with us to Chiswick tonight, instead. Now, I must send a letter to Mr. Brown at once by express messenger."

Accompanied by a dubious Lestrade, Holmes and Watson set off for Chiswick at eleven. As they crouched outside Laburnum Villa, they saw a dark figure open a window, enter the house, and emerge with a white object. The man was smashing it when Holmes leaped at him like a tiger, and in an instant Lestrade had handcuffed him. He was the man in the snapshot!

Holmes quickly but carefully examined each of the bust's fragments, holding it up to the light, but none was unusual.

At the London police station a search of Beppo's clothing revealed nothing but a long knife recently stained with blood.

"You will find," said Lestrade, "that my theory of the ruthless political group will work. I thank you for Beppo, Mr. Holmes."

"Come round at six tomorrow, Lestrade. I shall show you that even now you have not grasped the meaning of this business."

Holmes's theory of the case was different from Lestrade's, and he succeeded in proving it the next day. What was his theory?

Across

1 Agenda unit
5 Noncoms
9 Main mail centers: Abbr.
13 Adroit
14 Trifled
16 Branches
17 Soviet news agency
18 Sixteen drams
19 Drive out
20 Compass point
21 That: L.
22 Makes watertight
24 Narrated
26 Infirmary, for short
27 Diarist Anaïs ____
28 Oversweet
29 Mouths
32 Demotes: Slang
35 Sedimental
36 ____ canto
37 Rara ____
38 Prima donna Beverly

39 After-dinner candy
40 ____ of the first water
41 Grows
42 "____ be young was very heaven!"
43 Vitality
44 Day times: Abbr.
45 Between uno and tres
46 One of Esau's wives
47 ". . . I ____ multitudes."
51 It will out
54 Bewilderment
55 Card game
56 Infertile
57 Silly
59 Four gills
60 Relinquish
61 Lucifer
62 ____ of all right
63 Observer
64 Buddies
65 Rich, in Granada

Down

1 Between: Comb. form
2 Annoyer
3 Gear for van Gogh
4 Vernon and Vesuvius: Abbr.
5 "____ sweets are best."
6 U.S. financier
7 English river
8 Cabinet member, for short
9 ____ therapy
10 Bunyan
11 Siberian city
12 "____ the wind in that corner?"
15 Boils down
21 "____ an ancient Mariner . . ."
23 Pallid
25 Social insects
26 Rome has seven
28 Exasperates
29 News item
30 Schism
31 Voice range

32 Pouches
33 Eye part
34 Nitwit
35 Kind of sense
38 Hunting expeditions
39 Obligation
41 Walk in water
42 Off-white
45 Sets of twelve
46 Poisonous snake
47 Marking on Mars
48 Excuse
49 Kind of capital
50 "To be, or ____ be . . ."
51 Spice
52 Harold ____ , U.S. chemist
53 Roller coaster, e.g.
54 Computer input
58 Siesta
59 Face value of stocks

Puzzle XVII:
The Adventure of the Six Napoleons

Solution and epilogue on page 156

Solution and epilogue on page 156

— —
51 Across   24 Across   50 Down

— — — — — —, — — — — — — — — — — — — — ; — — — — —
9 Down   42 Across   32 Across   35 Down

— — — — — — — — — — — — — — — — — — — —
39 Down   47 Across   5 Down   28 Across

— — — — — — — — — — — — — — — — — — — —.
1 Across   29 Across   5 Down   40 Across

109

The Adventure of the Three Students

Sherlock Holmes hoped, when he and Dr. Watson arrived for a short stay at a university town in the fall of '95, that he could pursue his object—research into early English charters—without interruption. He was somewhat annoyed, Watson noted, when he received one evening a visit from an acquaintance, Mr. Hilton Soames, tutor at the College of St. Luke's. Soames, a tall, spare, nervous man, was in a state of great agitation.

"What a happy chance that you are here now, Mr. Holmes!" he cried. "We have had a very painful incident at St. Luke's."

"I should prefer that you call in the police," said Holmes.

"No, no, we must avoid scandal! Let me explain. Examinations for the valuable Fortescue Scholarship start tomorrow. My subject is Greek. I prepared a long passage for the candidates to translate—the text is secret. This afternoon the printer delivered the proofs. At four-thirty I had to leave to take tea with a friend, and I left the proofs on my writing table. I was absent about an hour. When I returned I was amazed to see a key in my door. Only my servant, Bannister—who's been with me ten years—has a duplicate; it was he, indeed, who had forgotten his key in the door. Someone had rummaged among the proofs' three pages. I had left them together, but now one was on the floor, one on a table near the window, and the third on my writing table.

"Bannister fell ill and collapsed in a chair when he saw what had happened. I gave him brandy, and then examined the room. On the window table I found pencil shavings and a piece of lead."

"Excellent!" said Holmes, his interest aroused.

"This was not all. My writing table has a leather surface—I discovered a cut in it three inches long! And on it I also found a pellet of black clay. Mr. Holmes, we must find the man. If the examination is postponed, a hideous scandal will ensue."

"I shall look into it," said Holmes, rising and putting on his coat. "Did anyone visit you after the proofs came?"

"Daulat Ras, an Indian student who lives on the same stair; he is entered in the examination. But I had not as yet unrolled the proofs, and only the printer knew when they would be delivered."

"Well," said Holmes, "let us go. You come too, Watson."

Soames's rooms were on the ground floor of the ancient building. Above were three students, one on each story. The tutor's study had a high latticed window facing the court; Holmes had to stand tiptoe with neck craned to look into the room.

On entering, Holmes examined the proofs. "No fingerprints," said he. "You left Bannister in a chair, you say? Ah, this one by the window table. Now, let us see. The man took the pages, one by one, from the writing table to the window table—here he could see if you came across the court. Oh!—

"Holmes had to stand tip-toe to look in."

you used the side door. So—he was copying the second page when your return forced him to a hasty retreat. Did you hear feet running up the stairs?"

"No, I can't say that I did," said Soames.

"And here are the pencil shavings and the lead—shavings dark blue, lead above usual size, silver letters NN on shavings indicate the maker to be Johann Faber. Now for the writing table. This small pellet is, I presume, the black clay you spoke of. Roughly pyramidal and hollowed out. Very interesting! And the cut in your table—a positive tear. It begins with a scratch and ends in a jagged hole. That door—I assume it leads to your bedroom. I should like to have a glance round. What a charming, old-fashioned room! And you hang your clothes behind this curtain? Someone could easily hide behind it. Halloa! What's this?"

Holmes stooped suddenly, and picked up a small clay pyramid, exactly like the other. "Your visitor *was* hiding here! When you came back, he caught up anything which would betray him, rushed in here, and stayed until you, and then Bannister, left. You say there are three students who use this stair and pass your door? Tell me about those who are in for the examination."

"They are all in," said Soames. "On the first floor is Gilchrist, a fine scholar and athlete. He got his Blue for the long jump. His father was the notorious Sir Jabez, who ruined himself on the turf, but my scholar is industrious, and will do well.

"Daulat lives on the second floor. He is quiet, inscrutable, but well up on his work—though his Greek is his weak subject.

"The top floor belongs to Miles McLaren, a brilliant fellow, but dissipated and unprincipled. He has been idling all this term, and he must look forward with dread to the examination."

"May I see Bannister," said Holmes, returning to the study.

Bannister was summoned. He was a little, white-faced, grizzled fellow of fifty, his face still twitching nervously.

"I understand that you left your key in the door," said Holmes.

"Yes, sir. I brought Mr. Soames's tea, but he was gone."

"And you fell ill when you saw the result of your carelessness. Where were you standing when you began to feel bad?"

"Where was I, sir? Why, here, near the door."

"That is singular, because you sat down in that chair by the window. Why did you pass these other chairs?"

"I don't know, sir. It didn't matter to me where I sat."

"You stayed here when your master left?"

"Only for a minute. I locked the door and went to my room."

"You have not mentioned anything to the three gentlemen?"

"No, sir—not a word. I haven't seen any of them."

When Bannister had left, Holmes asked Soames if he and Watson might visit the three students. "But no names, please!"

"It is not unusual for visitors to go over the oldest rooms in the college," said Soames. "We shall have no difficulty."

Gilchrist was a pleasant, tall, slim young fellow, who lent Holmes a pencil to copy some of the room's medieval elements.

The Indian, a silent, little fellow, also lent Holmes a pencil. Neither his nor Gilchrist's matched the pencil shavings.

But McLaren would allow no one in. "You can go to blazes!" he roared through the door. "Tomorrow is the exam, I'm busy!"

"A rude fellow," said Soames, flushing with anger.

"Can you tell me his exact height?" asked Holmes.

"Really, I can't say. He is taller than Daulat, but not so tall as Gilchrist. I suppose five foot six would be about it."

"Well, Mr. Soames," said Holmes, as he and Watson prepared to leave, "do not postpone the examination. We shall find a way out of your difficulty. I will take the black clay and the pencil cuttings with me. I shall drop round early in the morning."

The four stationers in town did not have a pencil to match the cuttings. Holmes shrugged off the clue's failure to lead anywhere. "I have little doubt we can build up a case without it," he said. After dinner, he sat lost in thought for a long time.

"Watson," said Holmes the next morning at eight, "it is time we went to St. Luke's. I have solved the mystery. I just put in two hours of hard work and covered five miles. Look!"

On his palm were three little pyramids of black clay.

"Why, Holmes, you had only two yesterday!"

"No. 3 came from the same source as the others. Come along."

"Thank heaven you have come," cried Soames. "What am I to do?"

"We must conduct a court-martial," said Holmes. "Watson, you sit here—you there, Soames. Kindly ring for Bannister."

Bannister entered, and shrank back in evident fear.

"Now, Bannister," said Holmes, "will you please tell us the truth about yesterday's incident?"

"I have told you everything, sir."

"Well, then, I must make a suggestion to you. When you sat down on that chair yesterday, you did so to conceal some object which would have shown who had been in the room."

"No, sir," said Bannister, whose face had turned ghastly white.

"It is only a suggestion," said Holmes. "I admit I am unable to prove it. But it seems probable enough, since as soon as Mr. Soames left, you released the man hiding in the bedroom."

"There was no man, sir," said Bannister in sullen defiance.

"I am afraid you have not spoken the truth. Now, Soames, will you kindly bring young Gilchrist down to join us."

Holmes had made three deductions, all of which pointed to Gilchrist's guilt. Holmes believed that only a student who had seen through Soames's window the proofs unrolled on the table would have risked entering. Only Gilchrist was tall enough; it must have been he. But this was no proof. From the fact that Gilchrist was a long-distance jumper, and from clues in Soames's rooms, Holmes had made two other deductions based on stronger evidence. From the clues, can you guess what Holmes's two deductions were?

Across

1 Watering places
5 Kind of beer
10 Deck post for cables
14 Hebrew letter
15 Corn breads
16 Greenland settlement
17 Rowers
18 Grant-____ (researcher's subsidy)
19 Red pigment
20 Wild silkworm
21 Card game
22 "Little Orphant Annie" poet
23 Cut
25 French silk
27 ____ Alamos
28 ____ grace (sinned)
32 Quarrel
35 Author of *Oliver's Story*
36 "Long, Long ____"
37 Astringent
38 ____ these days

39 Sourpuss
40 ____-jongg
41 Extra seed-coats
42 Sharpened
43 Royal tombs of Egypt
45 Cadge: Slang
46 Basketball basket
47 Kind of bean
51 Sorceress
54 ____ noire
55 Jane or John
56 Rake
57 Commandment word
59 Dr. Jekyll's alter ego
60 ____ instant (like a shot)
61 Postpone indefinitely
62 Founder of Troy
63 Tepee
64 Halts
65 Otherwise

Down

1 Loafers, e.g.
2 Shade of gray
3 Entrance courts
4 Requests for silence
5 Ears of grain
6 Single-celled organism
7 Med. student's subj.
8 Garland
9 Psychedelic drug
10 Beyond ____ (incredible)
11 Kind of type: Abbr.
12 *You Can't* ____ *It With You*
13 As ____ say
21 Boutique
22 Moon valley
24 Severe criticism
25 Utah State flowers
26 Patron saint of Norway
28 ____ one's way (gropes)
29 Parade's nemesis
30 Give the eye
31 Matrix

32 Cornmeal porridge
33 Some feet are made of it
34 German river
35 Derisive
38 Beginning, for short
39 Partner of circumstamce
41 Oriental nurse
42 Scottish philosopher
44 Brogue, for example
45 Small mesas
47 Fruit gelatin
48 Short pastoral poem
49 Complication
50 "All our ____ are swans."
51 Legal document
52 Feminine name
53 Mister, in Malaya
54 ____ au rhum
57 Louis and Lawrence
58 Panama
59 Hasten

Puzzle XVIII:
The Adventure of the Three Students

1	2	3	4	■	5	6	7	8	9	■	10	11	12	13
14				■	15					■	16			
17				■	18					■	19			
20			■	21			■		22					
23			24				■	25	26			■		
■		27			■	28					29	30	31
32	33	34		■	35				■	36			
37			■	38				■	39				
40		■	41				■	42					
43		44			■	45				■			
■	46			■	47			48	49	50
51	52	53		■	54			■	55			
56			■	57	58			■	59			
60			■	61			■	62			
63			■	64			■	65			

Solution and epilogue on page 157

1) __ __ __ __ __ __ __ __ __ __ __ __ __ __ __ __ __ __

   5 Across   33 Down   43 Across

__ __ __ __ __ __ __ __ __ __ __ __ __ __ __ __ __ ,

28 Across   47 Across   1 Down

__ __ __ __ __ __ .   2) __ __ __ __ __ __ __ __ __ __ __ __ ,

5 Down   38 Across   1 Down

__ __ __ __ __ __ __ __ __ __ __ __ __ __ __ __ __ __ .

5 Down   23 Across   61 Across

The Adventure of the Golden Pince-Nez

Sherlock Holmes and Dr. Watson were surprised, one stormy night in November of '94, to hear a cab splash up to their door. The caller was young detective Stanley Hopkins of Scotland Yard.

"I have come straight here from Yoxley Old Place," said Hopkins. "A young man named Willoughby Smith was murdered there this morning—but there seems to be no reason for the crime."

"Let us hear about it," said Holmes, lighting his cigar.

"Yoxley Old Place is a country house near Chatham in Kent. Professor Coram, an elderly invalid who keeps to his bed, has been there for some years. Mrs. Marker, the housekeeper, and Susan Tarlton, the maid, have been with him since his arrival. The professor, who is writing a book, recently hired young Smith, a Cambridge graduate of excellent character, as secretary—after two others had proved unsatisfactory. You could not find a more self-contained household. Smith knew nobody in the area; the others rarely left the premises. But the garden gate, a hundred yards from the main road, is kept open, and anyone may walk in.

"At eleven-thirty this morning Susan Tarlton was upstairs in the front bedroom, Professor Coram was in his bedroom, and Mrs. Marker was in the back of the house. At that moment Susan heard young Smith descend to the study immediately below her. A minute later there was a terrible scream in the study. The maid ran downstairs, and found Smith lying on the floor near the professor's desk, blood pouring from a wound in the underside of his neck. The stab had been made with a small knife which lay beside him. The knife was part of the fittings of the desk.

"At first the maid thought Smith was dead, but he opened his eyes for an instant. 'The professor,' he murmured—'it was she.' Susan swears that those were his exact words. Then he fell back dead. Mrs. Marker came on the scene a moment later. The professor was very upset; he can give no explanation for Smith's words.

"The killer must have entered the house by coming up the garden path to the back door, which opens into a corridor leading directly to the study. Any other way would have been too complicated. The escape must have been made the same way. There are two other exits from the study, but one, to the left of the desk, was blocked by Susan as she ran downstairs, and the other, at right angles to the back-door corridor, leads into another corridor and a staircase straight to the professor's room, which has only the one door. There were no footmarks on the garden path, despite the recent rain. This is the path that goes to the main road—the road was all mire. But someone had passed along the narrow grass border that lines the path. It must have been the murderer, since no one else had been there."

"Were the tracks on the grass border coming or going?"

"Impossible to say—there was no clear outline. Also, the corridor is lined with coconut matting; it takes no impression.

"The large desk, the main article in the study, consists of a writing table with a fixed bureau. The bureau has a double column of drawers, with a cupboard between them. The drawers were unlocked, but the cupboard was locked, as it contains important papers—but there was no sign of tampering, and nothing is missing." Hopkins paused. "Here is the most important piece of evidence—the police found it in Smith's hand." He produced a golden pince-nez, with two broken ends of silk cord. "Smith's sight was perfect. These must have been snatched from the assassin."

Holmes examined the pince-nez with great care and interest. "These glasses belong to a woman of refinement," said he. "They are unusually strong; the lady's vision is extremely contracted. Well, I suppose, Hopkins, you will want us to come out tomorrow."

Arriving at Yoxley Old Place with Watson and Hopkins the next morning, Holmes examined the grass strip along the garden path.

"Yes, someone did walk here," he said. "Our lady picked her steps carefully, since on one side she would leave tracks on the path, and on the other even clearer ones on the soft bed. You say she came back this way, Hopkins? A remarkable performance!"

In the study, Holmes observed, "If murder was in her mind, she would have brought a weapon. And how long was she here?"

"Mrs. Marker was tidying here ten minutes before the crime."

"Ah," said Holmes. Then—"What's this? A fresh scratch in the varnish near the bureau keyhole! Did you see this, Hopkins?"

"Yes, but you'll always find scratches round a keyhole."

Mrs. Marker was summoned. A sad-faced, elderly woman, she stated that the scratch had not been there the day before.

"We make progress," said Holmes, "Smith surprised our lady at the bureau. He seized her. She snatched up the knife and stabbed him. Then she escaped, with or without the object she came for. I should like to meet the professor now. Halloa, Hopkins, the professor's corridor is also lined with a coconut mat! You don't see the bearing on the case? I won't insist on it."

The professor's room overflowed with books. On the bed was a gaunt, dark-eyed man with white hair, smoking a cigarette.

"A smoker, Mr. Holmes?" asked Coram, with a curious accent. "Pray take a cigarette. I import them from Alexandria."

Holmes lit a cigarette as he darted glances over the room.

While the professor rambled on about Smith's tragic end and the interruption of his work, Holmes rapidly smoked cigarette after cigarette, pacing up and down one side of the room.

"Professor Coram, what do you think 'it was she' meant?"

"Susan misunderstood; the words are meaningless. Smith's death may have been accidental, or probably a suicide because of an affair of the heart.

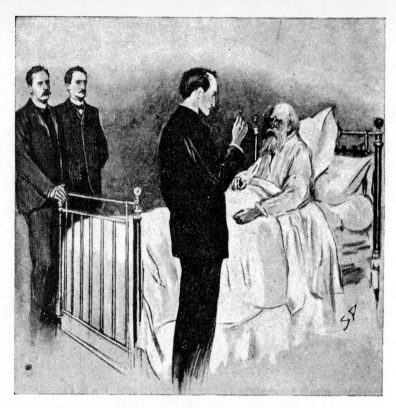

"Holmes took the key and examined it."

The pince-nez? A love-gage, no doubt."

"And what is in the cupboard of the bureau?" asked Holmes.

"My poor wife's letters. Here is the key, look for yourself."

Holmes took the key, examined it, and then handed it back.

"No, it won't help me," he said. "I shall go down to the garden to think about your suicide theory. We shall be back at two."

As they walked in the garden, Watson asked, "Have you a clue?"

"The cigarettes will show me," was all Holmes would say.

At lunch, Holmes looked up with great interest when Susan, who was serving, said that Smith had gone for a walk on the road the previous morning, returning a half hour before he was killed.

"Well, Mr. Holmes, have you solved the mystery?" asked the professor when Holmes, Watson and Hopkins came up at two o'clock. He handed Holmes his cigarette box, which Holmes clumsily dropped to the carpet. They all bent down to retrieve the cigarettes.

"Yes," said Holmes, as he straightened up. "The lady is here, in this room. You aided her to escape."

"You are mad, insane!" cried Coram. "Where is she now?"

"There," said Holmes, pointing to a high bookcase in a corner of the room. At that instant the bookcase swung round on a hinge, and a woman rushed into the room, crying in a strange foreign voice, "You are right!" Her plain face streaked with grime, she was blinking in near blindness, but there was nobility in her bearing. Stanley Hopkins quietly claimed her as his prisoner.

"I killed the young man accidentally," she said. "I only wanted him to let me go." She looked very ill. "I am this old wretch's wife; he was fifty and I twenty when we married in Russia. We were Nihilists; an officer was killed. To save his life and to earn a great reward, my husband betrayed his wife and his comrades. I was sent to Siberia. Among the Brotherhood, one was innocent—Alexis, the friend of my heart. He had written us letters dissuading us from violence. Those letters would have saved him. So would my diary—which also told of my love. My husband found and hid the diary, and the letters. Villain! Alexis is still in Siberia.

"I traced my husband, engaged a detective—he was your second secretary, Sergius. He found the papers in the cupboard, gave me an impression of the key and a plan of the house. He would go no further. I got the papers—but at what cost! On the road I had asked the young man to direct me, not knowing who he was."

"Yes!" cried Holmes. "The secretary told his master of the woman he had met. That was the meaning of 'it was she.' "

"Let me speak," said the woman. "I chose the wrong door and found myself in this room. I told Sergius if he would give me to the law, I would give him to the Brotherhood. It was agreed that when the police here left, I should slip away." She tore a small packet from her dress. "Here—save Alexis! And now—"

"Stop her!" cried Holmes. She held a small vial in her hand.

"Too late!" she said. "I took the poison in my hiding place."

Several clues had led Holmes to Mrs. Coram's hiding place. What was the first important clue that set him on the right track?

Across

1 Walked on
5 Airfield runway
10 Watered liquor
14 Alas!
15 _____ to (without limit)
16 Stratagem
17 "Oh, to _____ England . . ."
18 Venetian-blind units
19 Theatre org.
20 _____ on (attended)
22 Netherlands city
23 Organic compound
24 Medea, for example
27 At the age of: L. abbr.
30 Marsupial, in Melbourne
31 "Theirs _____ to reason why . . ."
32 WW II paramilitary agency
35 Specs
37 Beautify
39 Equally
40 Bar legally
41 Lowest limit
44 Sans
46 Suffix meaning "vegetable enzyme"
47 Man's nickname
48 Black cuckoo
49 School org.
50 "Her _____ are many . . ."
53 "I _____ a tale unfold . . ."
56 Capuchin monkey
57 Castile, saddle, etc.
61 _____ it (hit upon a solution)
62 Gig
64 Russian river
65 All right
66 39.37 inches
67 Healthy: Sp.
68 Olive and family
69 Tic
70 Redact

Down

1 Keep _____ on (watch closely)
2 Mother of Zeus
3 Pass over
4 Cotton cloth named for Nîmes
5 U.S. Navy Seamen, for short
6 Cities in Ohio and Spain
7 Author of *The Cloister and the Hearth*
8 Apprentice
9 Law-enforcement agencies: Abbr.
10 Snake in the _____
11 Littlest of the litter
12 Bone: Comb. form
13 Out of _____ (in disrepair)
21 Nanny
23 Philosophy of art
25 Caviar
26 Countless years
27 Chameleon's cousin
28 One-time immigrants' island
29 French historian
32 Out in front
33 Reconnoiter
34 Nose partitions
36 Alpine gear
38 Fine lava
42 Samovar
43 Faux pas
44 Hawaiian women
45 Animal order: Suffix
50 Weavers' reeds
51 _____ minute (hold on)
52 What Jack built
53 Half of a child's train
54 Like acorn's product
55 Pertaining to a grape
58 Jack-in-the-pulpit, for example
59 Madame, in Warsaw
60 Kind of machine
62 College degrees
63 Logo: Abbr.

Puzzle XIX:
The Adventure of the Golden Pince-Nez

Solution and epilogue on page 158

—— —— —— —— —— —— —— —— —— —— —— —— —— ——— , —— —— —— —— —— —— —

44 Across   **35 Across**   **24 Across**

—— —— —— —— —— —— —— —— —— —— —— —— —— —— —— ——

            53 Across   **31 Across**   **61 Across**   **1 Across**

—— —— —— —— —— —— —— —— —— —— —— —— —— —— —— —— — —

10 Down   **5 Across**   **44 Across**   **43 Down**

—— —— —— —— ; —— —— —— —— —— —— —— —— —— —— —— —— —— .

            53 Across   **17 Across**   **52 Down**

The Case of George Edalji

*P*Conan Doyle, a man of enormous energy and moral passion, was often involved in the fight against injustice. "It's every man's business to see justice done," said Sherlock Holmes. It was this conviction that led Doyle to take up the cause of George Edalji.

Browsing through a newspaper in 1906, Doyle read Edalji's own convincing story of his unjust imprisonment. Accused of disemboweling a pony in a field near his home on a dark, rainy night in 1903, Edalji, a young lawyer, had been sentenced to seven years' hard labor. After serving three years, he was released without explanation or vindication, and with a ruined career.

Doyle was determined first to prove Edalji's innocence, and then to find the actual perpetrator. He was burning with wrath at a miscarriage of justice based on racial prejudice: Edalji was the dark-skinned son of a Parsee (Hindu) Anglican priest.

Trouble had begun for the Reverend Edalji's family, who lived in a village north of Birmingham, when they received in 1892 a series of venomous, anonymous letters threatening death. The Hindu family was regarded with suspicion by some of the villagers; George, a quiet young boy, had bulging eyes—a sure sign of evil.

For three years the letters plagued the Edaljis, then suddenly stopped. During this time the key to the grammar school in the nearby town of Walsall was found on the Edaljis' doorstep; George was suspected of stealing it. Captain George Anson, the county's Chief Constable, who disliked the Edaljis, hinted that George had also written the letters, but no formal charge was made.

During the year 1903 sixteen animals in the area were disemboweled. The gory murders occurred at night; the police set up watch in vain. Anonymous letters appeared again, this time also sent to the police, accusing George Edalji of being the leader of a gang that had committed the atrocities.

Under Captain Anson's watchful eye, George was arrested for the pony's death; he was tried and convicted on flimsy evidence:

● The reverend's stained razors, found by the police when they searched the Edalji home; the stains turned out to be rust.

● George's damp jacket, which had two small stains of mammalian blood; the stains were dry, not fresh.

● George's muddied boots and trousers; George swore that the mud had been picked up that rainy night on a trip to a bootmaker in the next town, and the bootmaker corroborated this.

● A handwriting expert who testified that Edalji had written the anonymous letters branding himself a killer.

Doyle used the analytical and deductive methods of his own Sherlock Holmes to unravel the case:

- He met George Edalji, discovered he was so myopic as to be nearly blind (Doyle had been an opthalmologist), and concluded it was ridiculous to believe that such a man could slit a horse's stomach on a Stygian night, while eluding the police who had the Edaljis' house under constant surveillance.

- It was equally unbelievable that a man committing so bloody a crime would wind up with only two coin-sized stains on his jacket; the stains could have been made by a splash of gravy.

- Doyle also visited the scene of the crime; whereas the mud on George's boots had been black, the mud in the field was reddish.

Doyle's eloquent articles in *The Daily Telegraph* soon made the Edalji cause famous. As public sentiment for redress grew, Home Secretary Gladstone appointed a commission of three to look into the matter (a Court of Criminal Appeal did not yet exist).

The commission reported that the verdict was not supported by the evidence, but that Edalji, having misled the police with his anonymous letters, did not deserve vindication or damages. An interesting aspect of the Gladstone Commission was *the naming of Captain Anson's second cousin as one of its three members*.

Conan Doyle persisted. He consulted the handwriting expert in the Dreyfus trial, and with his help traced the anonymous letters to a former, delinquent student of the Walsall Grammar School. Doyle's strong suspect had left the area in 1895 and returned in 1903, during which time he had been apprenticed to a butcher and the poison-pen letters had ceased.

But Doyle's new evidence was not officially accepted. Although the Law Society cleared Edalji, so that he could resume his career, and *The Daily Telegraph* called for a retrial, the Home Secretary would go no further; to this extent Doyle failed.

Disappointed, Doyle blamed "officialdom" standing "solid together." But his fight to see justice done helped point up the need for a Court of Criminal Appeal, which was created in 1907.

The Adventure of the Missing Three-Quarter

It was not uncommon for weird telegrams to arrive at Baker Street, but one gloomy February morning Sherlock Holmes received one that he and Dr. Watson found fairly incomprehensible.

Please await me. Terrible misfortune. Right wing three-quarter missing, indispensable tomorrow. Overton

The telegram was soon followed by its sender, Cyril Overton of Trinity College, Cambridge, an enormous young man, sixteen stone of bone and muscle, whose face was haggard with anxiety.

"Inspector Hopkins advised me to come to you," said Overton. "It's awful, Mr. Holmes! Godfrey Staunton, the crack three-quarter—you've heard of him, of course—the hinge that the whole team turns on, whether it's passing, or tackling, or dribbling—he's missing! We are undone unless you can find him."

"Godfrey Staunton is a new name to me," said Holmes.

Overton was shocked. "Then you don't know me either!"

Holmes shook his head good-humoredly.

"Great Scott!" cried the athlete. "I was first reserve for England against Wales, and I've skippered the Varsity Rugger team all this year. Mr. Holmes, where *have* you lived?"

"You live in a sweeter and healthier world than I do," said Holmes. "Now, my good sir, how can I help you?"

"Tomorrow we play Oxford," said Overton. "Yesterday we came up to London and settled at Bentley's hotel. At ten last night I went round to see if all the fellows had gone to roost. Godfrey seemed bothered, but said it was just a headache. Half an hour later, the porter tells me that a man with a beard called with a note for Godfrey. The porter took it up, and when Godfrey read it, he fell back in a chair as though he had been pole-axed. Then he went downstairs where the man was waiting, and the two of them went off together. Godfrey would not let his skipper down if he could help it. I wired to Cambridge—no one has seen him there. And I wired to Lord Mount-James, but have had no reply."

"Lord Mount-James," said Holmes, "is one of the richest men in England. What is Staunton's relation to him?"

"Godfrey is an orphan. Lord Mount-James is his nearest relative—his uncle. The old man's a miser, but Godfrey is his heir."

"This throws new light on the matter," said Holmes. "I strongly recommend that you make your preparations for the match without Staunton. What tore him away, will likely keep him away. Let us step round together to the hotel."

The porter described Staunton's caller as a "medium-looking chap" of fifty, who also seemed very agitated. He had overheard only one word of the few that the two had exchanged—"time."

"Did you take any other messages to Staunton during the day?"

"A telegram, at six o'clock, sir. I waited till he wrote an answer, but then he took it himself. What did he write it with? Why, with a pen, sir."

"Then I think," said Holmes, "we will find some impression on this blotting pad. Ah, yes, this is the very thing!"

He tore off a strip of the blotting paper, turned it to the reverse side, and they all read: "Stand by us for God's sake!"

"Staunton saw a great danger ahead from which someone could protect him," said Holmes. "Another person is involved—mark the 'us.' We must find out to whom the telegram was addressed. Meanwhile, Mr. Overton, in your presence, I wish to go through these papers on the desk. Hum, you say your friend was healthy—I think he had some secret trouble. May I have these papers?"

"One moment!" cried a querulous voice. A queer little old man, dressed in rusty black, had appeared in the doorway. "Who are you, and by what right do you touch Mr. Staunton's papers?"

"I am a private detective, engaged by Mr. Overton here."

"I am Lord Mount-James, and don't look to me for a penny!"

"It is possible," said Holmes, "that a gang of thieves have taken your nephew to find out about your house and your habits."

"Heavens, I didn't think of that! Spare no pains, Mr. Detective. You can count on me for a fiver, or even a tenner!"

The next stop for Holmes and Watson was the nearest telegraph office. "I sent a telegram yesterday," said Holmes to the young lady in charge, "but have had no reply. I may not have signed it."

"To whom was it addressed?" she asked.

Holmes put his finger to his lips and glanced at Watson. "The last words were 'for God's sake,' " he whispered confidentially.

"This is it," said she, putting the telegram on the counter.

"As I thought, no signature," said Holmes. "Many thanks."

Outside, Holmes said, "Our destination now is Cambridge, where we will visit Dr. Leslie Armstrong, to whom the wire was sent."

"He is head of the University's medical school," said Watson.

It was dark when they reached the old university city. The granite-jawed, brooding-eyed doctor, who lived in a mansion on a busy thoroughfare, received them with displeasure.

"I have heard of you, Mr. Holmes," said he, "and am aware of your profession—one of which I by no means approve."

"Then you are in agreement with every criminal in the country."

"I refer to your raking up the secrets of private individuals."

"I endeavor to prevent exposure of private matters—the police cannot," said Holmes. "Can you tell me where Godfrey Staunton is, and why he paid

"'One moment!' cried a querulous voice."

you this large bill last month?"

Dr. Armstrong's dark face turned crimson with fury.

"I'll trouble you to leave, sir," he said. "Tell your employer, Lord Mount-James, that I want nothing to do with his agent."

A pompous butler ushered Holmes and Watson to the door.

"Here we are—stranded," said Holmes, laughing. "That inn just opposite Armstrong's house is singularly well situated. Engage a front room, Watson, while I make a few inquiries."

Holmes returned late, covered with dust, and dejected. The sound of carriage wheels brought him to the window.

"The doctor's brougham has been out three hours," he said. "That gives us a radius of ten or twelve miles, and he goes at least once or twice a day. I learned this from a friendly native; Armstrong's coachman set a dog on me.

Armstrong is not a doctor in practice—whom does he visit? I engaged a bicycle and followed the carriage, but he noticed me, got out, and sardonically let me go ahead. I went on for a few miles, and waited for him, but he gave me the slip. I do not know if these journeys are connected to Staunton, but as the good doctor is so very keen to keep me from following, I shall not be satisfied until I have made the matter clear."

"We can follow him tomorrow," said Watson.

"No, Watson, Cambridgeshire scenery does not lend itself to concealment. I have wired Overton for any new developments."

The next morning brought Holmes an offensive letter from Dr. Armstrong, stating that Holmes was wasting his time in Cambridge.

"He knows where Staunton is—to that I'll now swear," said Holmes. "I must do some independent exploration today, and hope to bring back a more favorable report before evening."

Once more Holmes returned late, weary, and unsuccessful.

"I have visited all the villages in the general direction the doctor took yesterday, but no one has seen the daily appearance of a brougham and pair. The doctor has scored again. Is there a telegram for me from Overton?"

"Yes," said Watson. "I opened it. 'Ask for Pompey from Jeremy Dixon, Trinity College.' I don't understand it."

"It's in answer to a question from me. I'll just send a note to Mr. Dixon. Any news of the match?"

"Oxford won by a goal. Staunton was greatly missed."

Watson was horrified, the next morning, to see in Holmes's hand a hypodermic syringe. Holmes laughed at his dismay.

"No, no, my dear fellow, no cause for alarm. This will be the key that will unlock our mystery. Eat a good breakfast, Watson, for I propose to get on the doctor's trail today."

"In that case," said Watson, "we had best carry our breakfast with us, for his carriage is at the door."

"Never mind. Let him go. He will be clever, indeed, if he can drive where I cannot follow him."

This mystery has a very sad solution, one that even Holmes could not have deduced. But at this point, Holmes had figured out a way to trail Dr. Armstrong with the help of Pompey and the hypodermic syringe. Can you guess 1) who Pompey was, and 2) how Holmes used the syringe?

Across

1 Saltwater fish
5 Practical joker
10 Football player
14 Mexican dish
15 Stick out like ___ thumb
16 Sioux
17 Public utility, for short
18 Get an inkling of
19 Threefold
20 Heroine of *The Merchant of Venice*
22 Weird ones, as in *Macbeth*
24 Streak ___ luck
27 Spanish uncle
28 Bearing
31 Metrical foot
35 Sashes
36 U.S. industrialist
38 Guido's high note
39 "Arms and the ___ I sing."
40 Kind of horn

42 Tray, for example
43 Part of Congress: Abbr.
44 ___ q. t.
45 Wonderland creature
46 Clippers
48 Decal
51 Gymnastics gear
52 Ancient city in Latium
53 ___ fortune (fate)
57 Double-crowned sun hats
61 Sewing-machine inventor
62 Nettle plant
65 ___ the dirt
66 Finished
67 Writer Hoffer, and others
68 Margarine
69 Preachments: Abbr.
70 Ledger entry
71 Encounter

Down

1 Short distance
2 Aureole
3 Maple genus
4 Fishing flies
5 Melon
6 L. A. univ.
7 Kind of dance
8 Footed vases
9 Entreaty
10 Second half of an inning
11 To ___ (exactly)
12 Letters, for short
13 Knows: Scot.
21 "___ were a King . . ."
23 Chinese river
25 Traveling salesman
26 "To bring ___ a friend."
28 God of revelry
29 Disconcert
30 Flush

32 ___ roses
33 "The Man ___"
34 Julius Erving, for example
37 Rows
40 Horary
41 Not warehoused
45 Peter the Great's domain
47 Moslem princes
49 Bear witness
50 Never: Ger.
53 ___ who
54 ___ to (stopped)
55 Water jug
56 Passenger
58 Wing: Fr.
59 "Is this a dagger which ___ . . ."
60 Jigger
63 Playing marble
64 ___ on parle français

Puzzle XX:
The Adventure of the Missing Three-Quarter

1	2	3	4		5	6	7	8	9		10	11	12	13
14					15						16			
17					18						19			
20				21				22		23				
		24			25	26		27						
28	29	30						31			32	33	34	
35					36		37				38			
39				40	41						42			
43				44							45			
46			47				48		49	50				
			51				52							
53	54	55				56			57			58	59	60
61				62		63	64			65				
66				67						68				
69				70						71				

Solution and epilogue on page 159

1) __ __ __ __ __ __ __   __ __ __.   2) __ __ __ __

   40 Across   42 Across   60 Down

__ __ __ __ __   __ __ __ __ __   __ __ __ __ __   __ __ __ __ __ __   __ __

18 Across   66 Across   10 Across   53 Across

__ __ __ __ __ __ __,   __ __ __ __ __ __ __ __ __.

4 Down   28 Across

129

The Adventure of the Abbey Grange

It was not until Sherlock Holmes had hurried himself and Dr. Watson on to the early train for Kent, one wintry morning of '97, that he told Watson of the note he had received from Inspector Stanley Hopkins imploring his aid in solving the murder of Sir Eustace Brackenstall at the noble's estate, the Abbey Grange. But when they arrived at the wide, pillared house, set in a great park, young Hopkins met them with an apology.

"Since Lady Brackenstall has come to herself, she has given so clear an account of last night's affair that there is not much left for us to do. It was surely the work of the Randall gang, the father and two sons. They did a job near here at Sydenham a fortnight ago, but it's more than robbery this time. Lady Brackenstall is in the morning-room. I think you had best speak to her, and then we will examine the dining-room together."

Lady Mary Brackenstall was a blonde, blue-eyed woman of exquisite beauty, but over one eye rose a hideous swelling, which her maid, a tall, austere woman, was bathing. The lady wore a loose dressing-gown; a dinner-dress lay on the couch beside her. Hopkins asked her to tell her story to Holmes and Watson.

"It is no secret that my marriage of a year was not a happy one," said Lady Brackenstall. "Sir Eustace was a confirmed drunkard. But the fault may be partly mine; I was brought up in South Australia, and found the prim English life uncongenial.

"The dwelling-rooms in this house are in this central section; my maid Theresa's room is above mine. The servants sleep in the farther wing—the robbers must have known no sound could reach them there. Sir Eustace had retired about ten, and the servants were in their quarters. Only Theresa and I were up—she in her room, and I in here, reading. Before retiring I usually check the rooms in this part of the house. In the dining-room, as I approached the long French window, which is covered with a thick curtain, I suddenly felt the wind blow in. I flung the curtain aside, and found myself facing a large, elderly man, with two young men behind him. As I opened my mouth to scream, he struck me a savage blow over the eye, and I fell unconscious. When I came to, I found that they had torn down the bell-rope and secured me tightly to an oaken chair. A handkerchief bound my mouth.

"It was at that instant that my husband entered, carrying a cudgel in his hand. He rushed at the burglars, but the elderly man picked the poker out of the grate and struck him a horrible blow. He never moved again. I fainted, but only for a few minutes. When I opened my eyes I saw that the burglars had collected the silver from the sideboard, and had opened a bottle of wine which stood there. Each of them had a glass in his hand. Finally they withdrew, closing the window after them. When I got my mouth free, my screams brought Theresa, who called the police."

"'My marriage was not a happy one,' said Lady Brackenstall."

"May I now hear your experience?" asked Holmes of the maid.

"Sitting by my window, I saw three men down by the lodge gate before they came to the house," she said. "I thought nothing of it until I heard my mistress scream. I ran down to find Sir Eustace on the floor, his blood all over the room. That is all. And now my lady must get the rest she badly needs."

As Theresa led Lady Brackenstall from the room, Hopkins remarked, "Theresa has been with her all her life."

The dining-room was a huge, high chamber, with a carved oak ceiling, and a large, deep fireplace overhung with a massive oak mantelpiece. The crimson cord which had bound Lady Brackenstall had slipped to the floor, but was still knotted. The body of Sir Eustace, his handsome face convulsed with hatred, lay in front of the fire. Holmes examined the heavy, bent poker.

"The elder Randall must be a powerful man," he remarked. "But you should have no difficulty in getting him."

131

"None at all," said Hopkins. "But how could they have done so mad a thing, knowing that the lady could describe them? Perhaps they thought they had rendered her senseless. I have heard, by the way, that Sir Eustace was a good man when sober, but a perfect fiend when drunk—he once threw a decanter at Theresa. Between ourselves, it will be a brighter house without him."

Holmes was down on his knees, examining the knots in the red bell-rope, and scrutinizing the frayed, weakened end where it had snapped off when the burglar had pulled it down.

"The burglar must have been told no one would hear the bell ring in the kitchen," said Holmes. "You examined the servants?"

"Yes, they are all of excellent character," said Hopkins.

"What did the burglars take?"

"Some pieces of silver plate from the sideboard. They did not ransack the house, probably upset by Sir Eustace's death."

"Yet Lady Brackenstall saw them drinking wine," said Holmes. "What's this?" The three glasses were grouped together, tinged with wine, one of them containing some dregs of beeswing. "The glasses puzzle me. You see nothing remarkable, Hopkins? Well, let it pass. Come, Watson, it's time to take the train home."

But at the station, Holmes had a change of heart.

"I *can't* leave the case in this condition! It's all wrong! Those three wine-glasses. I should have examined the dining-room more carefully—perhaps have found something more definite. The lady's story is suspicious. Why murder a man, when three men are sufficient to overpower him? Why the limited plunder? And beeswing in only one glass. It means that two glasses were used and their dregs poured into the third, to give a false impression."

The household at the Abbey Grange were surprised by their return, but Holmes, finding that Hopkins had gone off, took possession of the dining-room, and devoted two hours to a laborious investigation. Finally, to Watson's astonishment, Holmes climbed up on to the mantelpiece. Far above his head hung the few inches of red bell-rope which were still attached to the wire. He rested his knee on a wooden bracket on the wall, and was thus able to bring himself almost within reach of the broken end of the rope. He sprang down with a cry of satisfaction.

"We have our man, Watson! Only one, but one very tall, strong as a lion, and remarkably quick-witted, for the whole story is his concoction. *Yet in that bell-rope he left a clue that proves Lady Brackenstall lied*. See the mark on the seat of the oaken chair? It is blood! If she were seated on the chair when the crime was done, how comes the mark? I'll wager her dinner-dress shows a corresponding mark. Now, I must speak with Theresa."

The maid did not attempt to conceal her hatred of her late employer. "He was all honey when they first met—Mary Fraser had just arrived in London from Australia. He won her with his title, his money, and his false London ways. We arrived in June, and they were married in January. Yes, you may see her now."

Lady Brackenstall received Holmes and Watson in the morning-room. "What do you want of me?" she asked.

"The truth," said Holmes. "Your story is a fabrication."

"I have told you all I know," she said firmly.

"I am sorry," said Holmes. He and Watson left the house.

There was a frozen pond in the park, with a single hole left for a solitary swan. Holmes gazed at it, then scribbled a note for Stanley Hopkins and left it with the lodge-keeper.

"Our next stop," said Holmes, "is the office of the Adelaide-Southampton line, which connects South Australia with England."

There they learned that on the passenger list for the line's ship arriving at England in June of '95 were Miss Fraser and her maid. The ship was now on its way to Australia, with the same officers, excepting one. Jack Croker had been promoted, and was soon to captain their new ship. He lived in Sydenham. His record was magnificent, but off-deck he was wild, hotheaded.

Holmes sent a telegram off, and he and Watson returned to Baker Street, where they received a visit from Stanley Hopkins.

"How on earth did you know the stolen silver was at the bottom of that pond?" he asked Holmes. "But I have had a bad setback. The Randall gang were arrested in New York this morning."

After Hopkins left, Holmes said, "I expect developments, Watson." And that evening, Captain Jack Croker, tall and handsome, came calling. He stood with clenched hands and heaving breast.

"Sit down," said Holmes. "Be frank with me or I'll crush you. The killer of Sir Eustace used sailors' knots to tie up Lady Mary, he made up an unbelievable story for her to tell, and he did not pull down the bell-rope, but was careless and left me the positive clue that I needed. Now, give us a *true* account of what happened."

What had the killer done with the bell-rope that gave Holmes his clue?

Across

1 Henry James's biographer
5 Leap
10 Ancient Asian kingdom
14 Astor or Bountiful
15 Out of this world
16 Asiatic palm
17 Play down
19 Costly
20 Strap
21 Hwys.
22 Exclusively
23 ___ so (extremely)
25 Thor's wife
27 Kind of whale
31 Turtle genus
33 "___ till the sun excludes you . . ."
36 ___ Minor
37 Voyaging
39 New Zealand native
41 Torpor
43 "And still she ___ azure-lidded

sleep."
45 Kind of pneumonia
46 Ratio phrase
48 Capable of being: Suffix
49 Title for Joan of Arc: Abbr.
50 Hankering
52 Raveled
54 ___ polloi
55 This: Sp.
57 Kind of grass
60 Harvest
62 Rubbish
67 Acknowledge
68 Become ___ (take a liking to)
70 Headland
71 Indian statesman
72 Ancient Greek temple
73 Lollapalooza
74 Cash, for example
75 "___ it should come to this!"

Down

1 Hebrew month
2 Subject of Margrethe II
3 Old Norse poetry
4 Caustics
5 College degrees
6 Bizarre
7 Stumped
8 Old Greek musical note
9 Stylish
10 No ___ (without limit)
11 ___ Bien Phu
12 Semiprecious stone
13 Quite contrary one
18 Korean statesman
24 True: Fr.
26 "Woe ___ !"
27 Curly cabbages
28 ". . . but the end ___ yet."
29 Love, in Leipzig
30 Pasternak character
32 Mizzen

33 "O! swear ___ the moon . . ."
34 Papal cape
35 Like a harrow
38 Levantine vessel
40 Samoan port
42 Terzetto
44 Warehouse upper story
47 Closefitting dresses
51 Capital of Albania
53 Quickly, old style
54 Woodcutter
56 Extra
57 City on the Brazos
58 The Terrible one
59 ___ in (inveigle)
61 Summers, in France
63 Charter
64 Feminine name
65 Colonnade
66 "A ___ , of golden daffodils."
69 Snub

Puzzle XXI:
The Adventure of the Abbey Grange

1	2	3	4		5	6	7	8	9		10	11	12	13
14					15						16			
17				18							19			
20						21					22			
			23	24				25	26					
27	28	29	30				31	32				33	34	35
36					37	38				39	40			
41				42				43	44					
45					46	47				48				
49				50	51			52	53					
			54				55	56						
57	58	59			60	61				62	63	64	65	66
67					68			69						
70					71						72			
73					74						75			

Solution and epilogue on page 160

___ ___ ___ ___ ___ ___   ___ ___ ___ ___   ___ ___ ___ ___; ___ ___ ___ ___ ___ ___

27 Across   69 Down   59 Down   52 Across

___ ___ ___ ___ ___   ___ ___ ___   ___ ___ ___ ___   ___ ___ ___ ___ ___ ___ ___   ___ ___ ___ ___

22 Across   10 Down   59 Down   75 Across   5 Across

___ ___ ___ ___   ___ ___ ___ ___ ___ .   ___ ___ ___ ___   ___ ___ ___   ___ ___ ___ ___   ___ ___

14 Across   13 Down   10 Down   59 Down   68 Across

___ ___ ___ ___ ___ ___   ___ ___ ___ ___   ___ ___ ___   ___ ___ ___ ___ .

68 Across (continued)   57 Across   33 Across   52 Across

Baker Street Irregulars' Crossword Puzzle
A Challenging Treat for Holmes Buffs

Across

1 A treatise on this, written at the age of twenty-one, had a European vogue and earned its author a professorship. (2 words, 8, 7)

8 It was of course to see these that Holmes enquired the way from Saxe-Coburg Square to the Strand (2 words, 10, 5)

11 How the pips were set (2)

13 Not an Eley's No. 2 (which is an excellent argument with a gentleman who can twist steel pokers into knots) but the weapon in the tragedy of Birlstone (3)

14 What was done on the opposite wall in bullet-pocks by the patriotic Holmes (2)

15 What Watson recognized when he put his hand on Bartholomew Sholto's leg (5)

18 Where Watson met young Stamford, who introduced him to Sherlock Holmes (3)

20 A kind of pet, over which Dr. Grimesby Roylott hurled the local blacksmith (4)

21 Holmes should have said this before being so sure of catching the murderers of John Openshaw (2)

22 The kind of Pedro whence came the tiger (3)

23 Though he knew the methods, Watson sometimes found it difficult to do this (3)

25 Patron saint of Old Mr. Farquhar's affliction and perhaps of Abe Slaney's men (5)

27 Perhaps a measure of Holmes's chemicals (2)

28 In short, Watson (2)

29 ⚇ ⚇ (2)

30 Curious that he did nothing in the nighttime (3)

31 This would obviously not describe the empty house opposite 221b Baker Street (3)

34 It seems likely that Watson's elder brother suffered from this disease (2)

35 Though you might have taken this at Lodge 29, Chicago, nevertheless, you had to pass a test as well at Lodge 341, Vermissa (4)

37 The *Star* of Savannah (4)

40 Mrs. Barclay's reproach (in The Crooked Man, of course) suggests the parable of this (3)

41 Scrawled in blood-red letters across the bare plaster at No. 3, Lauriston Gardens (5)

43 Holmes found this, because he was looking for it in the mud (5)

44 Suggests Jonathan Small's leg (3)

45 The brother who left Watson no choice but to relate The Final Problem (2 words, 5, 8)

Down

1 A country district in the west of England where "Cooee" was a common signal (2 words, 8, 6)

2 Charles Augustus Milverton dealt with no niggard hand; therefore this would not describe him (4)

3 The kind of practice indulged in by Mr. Williamson, the solitary cyclist's unfrocked clergyman—"there was a man of that name in orders, whose career has been a singularly dark one." (3)

4 There is comparatively as much sense in Hafiz. Indeed, it's a case of

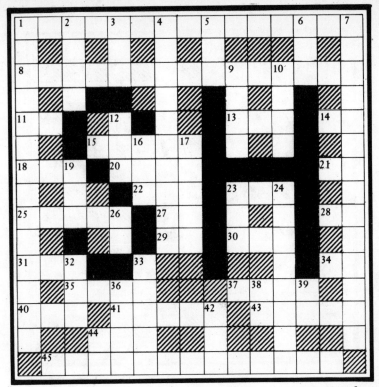

Solution on page 138

Solution on page 138

identity. (3 words, 2, 2, 6)

5 Caused the rift in the beryl coronet (3)

6 Many of Holmes's opponents had cause to (3)

7 Begins: "Whose was it?" "His who is gone." "Who shall have it?" "He who will come." (2 words, 8, 6)

9 of four (4)

10 The number of Napoleons plus the number of Randall gang (4)

12 One of the five sent "S.H. for J.O." (3)

16 To save the dying detective trouble, Mr. Culverton Smith was kind enough to give the signal by turning this up (3)

17 The blundering constable who failed to gain his sergeant's stripes in the Lauriston Gardens Mystery (5)

19 There was a giant one of Sumatra; yet it was unwritten (3)

23 How Watson felt after the Final Problem (3)

24 He was epollicate (8)

26 Initials of the second most dangerous man in London (2)

32 Though Miss Mary Sutherland's boots were not unlike, they were really odd ones; the one having this slightly decorated, and the other plain (3)

33 You may forgive the plural form of these tobaccos, since Holmes smoked so much of them (5)

36 Behind this Black Jack of Ballarat waited and smoked an Indian cigar, of the variety which are rolled in Rotterdam (4)

38 and 39 The best I can make of these is the Latin for the sufferers of the epidemic which pleased Holmes so extremely that he said "A long shot, Watson, a very long shot," and pinched the Doctor's arm (4)

42 One of the two in the cardboard box (3)

44 Initials of the street in which Mycroft lodged (2)

```
B I N O M I A L T H E O R E M   M
O E   A S U         U   U
S P A U L D I N G S K N E E S   G
C R     N   I   I           G
O   P H   G U N       V R
M R I G O R   N   E         A
B A R P A R A         D V
E A   S A N   S E E         E
V I T U S   C C A   N       D R
A     M E E   D O G         I T
L E T   S       I   D U
L O A T H       L O N E     U
E W E R A C H E   V E S T A L
Y   P E G     A       E
  J A M E S M O R I A R T Y
```

This delightful but difficult puzzle, which requires an intimate knowledge of the Holmes stories, first appeared in Christopher Morley's column in *The Saturday Review of Literature*, May 19, 1934, and was attributed to Mycroft Holmes, Sherlock's brilliant but lazy brother. To readers submitting the correct solution prior to its publication, Morley offered automatic membership in the Baker Street Irregulars, a group devoted to "the study of the Sacred Writings."

Mycroft Holmes.

138

Solutions & Epilogues

Puzzle I: *A Scandal in Bohemia*

```
A S P I C  ■  M U S T A N G
■ K E T T L E  ■  A N T O N I A
D R E S S E D  ■  N E A R I N G
D O M  ■  A R I L  ■  V I O L A S
E N S E  ■  I C E M E N  ■
■  S E C T I O N  ■  N I T A
R E A C T  ■  F O L L O W E D
A T C O U R T  S Y E N I T E
M A R R I E R S  ■  O A S E S
P L O T  ■  S E N S I N G  ■
■  R E T A I N  ■  E R I N
C H A L E T  ■  P L U M  ■  O R O
H O B A R T S  ■  T R E A T E D
E M E R A L D  ■  S E A S O N
F E L I N E S  ■  S N A R E
```

Holmes tore the letter open; the three men read it together.

My dear Mr. Sherlock Holmes:
 I realized I had betrayed the hiding place of the photograph. I knew if the King employed an agent it would be you. Trained as an actress, I quickly put on male costume, and followed the "clergyman" home to confirm my suspicions. My husband and I thought flight best, when pursued by an antagonist like you. As to the photograph, your client may rest in peace. I keep it only as a weapon against any steps he may take in the future. I love and am loved by a better man than he. I leave another photograph the King may want.

"What a woman!" cried the King. "Had she been on my level!"

"She seems on a very different level, your Majesty," said Holmes coldly. "I am sorry that I was not more successful."

"Her word is sacred!" the King cried. "Name your reward!"

To the King's amazement, Holmes asked only for the photograph of Irene—*the* woman whose mettle most nearly matched his own.

K	A	T	E	■	C	U	K	E	■	W	H	I	L	E
E	W	E	S	■	O	V	E	N	■	I	O	T	A	S
P	A	R	T	■	B	U	R	R	■	L	O	E	S	S
T	Y	R	O	■	U	L	N	A	■	S	K	A	T	E
■	■	N	O	R	A	■	P	R	O	A	■	■	■	■
B	A	S	I	N	G	■	S	T	A	N	H	O	P	E
E	T	T	A	S	■	S	T	U	N	■	S	U	R	E
A	Y	E	■	■	S	T	A	R	T	■	■	T	I	L
S	O	R	E	■	O	R	N	E	■	E	V	A	D	E
T	U	N	N	E	L	E	D	■	L	E	I	T	E	R
■	■	G	L	E	E	■	■	P	E	N	N	■	■	■
H	A	B	L	A	■	T	A	R	A	■	C	O	B	B
A	S	L	I	P	■	C	R	A	G	■	E	L	L	A
S	T	O	S	S	■	A	I	N	U	■	N	E	O	N
T	O	T	H	E	■	R	A	K	E	■	T	O	C	K

As Holmes and Watson set out in a hansom, followed by Jones and Merryweather, Watson asked where they were going, and why.

"To the Coburg bank, of which Merryweather is a director," said Holmes. "Vincent Spaulding is none other than John Clay, murderer and thief; I knew it was he from Wilson's description. My little reputation may be lost in explaining the rest, for I saw at once that the League was a ruse to get Wilson out of the way. Ross's red hair gave Clay the method—Ross is Clay's accomplice. Half wages indicated Clay's strong motive for working at Wilson's. What was it? I thought of Clay's trick of vanishing into the cellar. What down there would take so long to accomplish? Why, digging a tunnel to another building. The bank's location and the knees of Clay's trousers confirmed my suspicions."

"But how do you know that the bank will be robbed tonight?"

"The League's closing means that the tunnel is completed. I learned from Merryweather that the bank's cellar holds a shipment of French gold. Saturday would give the villains two days to escape, but they can't begin until Wilson is in bed. We'll wait for them; the gold will be safe, and Jones will get his man."

And so it was, to the last detail, as Holmes had predicted.

```
M A K E   . P E L F .   . E L K
A L I X . P A T I O . . U P O N
S T E P F A T H E R . . N E R O
S A V I O R . E B B . . W E N T
. . A R E A L . O R E . . . .
W A N T I N G . B R I D A L S
I R A E . T O K E E P . N E A
N E D D A . R I C . S I G N S
E T E . D E A D A S . M E T S
S E R M O N S . M I S P L A Y
. . A S H . A E M I A . .
S T A R . A H S . I N C O M E
H O L Y . N E W S L E T T E R
A N A S . C R A T E . E T N A
H E R . E O N S . D O E S
```

When Watson returned to Baker Street, the next evening, he queried Holmes about the solution to Mary's case, which Holmes had withheld to keep the good doctor in a bit of suspense.

"Be patient, my dear Watson. I expect Mr. Windibank at any moment. He has written that he would be here today at six. It was the typed signature on Angel's letters, of course, which was conclusive; he feared that his handwriting would be recognized. But there's no law to touch the scoundrel. Ah, here's Windibank."

A middle-sized fellow, about thirty years old, clean-shaven, sallow-skinned and sharp-eyed, entered and spoke up in an oily voice. "I am sorry that Miss Sutherland has troubled you about this matter, Mr. Holmes. Besides, how could you possibly find Mr. Angel?"

"I have found him, Mr. Windibank! The letter which you sent me to make your appointment was typed on the same machine as Angel's letters. Typewriters are as distinctive as handwriting!"

"It—it's not actionable," stammered Windibank.

"Alas, no. You and your wife connived in this despicable affair, and while the law cannot touch you I can—" and Holmes reached for his hunting crop. Windibank was gone in a flash.

```
B O T H █ A R A B S █ B A A
A G R I █ G E N O A █ S E L F
S P E D █ R A T O N █ T E A R
S U N D A E █ I N D U C T S █
█ E L E E █ E A R L █
H O B N A I L S █ L I A B L E
A H A █ I N D U E █ S I R E S
S A R I █ G E S T O █ R A G S
P R O N G █ R A N C H █ V E E
S E N D E R █ N A T A T O R S
█ O R E G █ S E T A █
█ C L O T H E S █ T H R E A T
W E A R █ E N A C T █ R A R E
A N D S █ A R G U E █ E V E R
S T Y █ T E S T S █ D E A N
```

"It's a theory until it's tested, Watson. Let's test it!"

They drove to the cells in Bow Street, where an inspector led them to the sleeping Boone. Holmes took out a bath sponge that he had brought from The Cedars, moistened it, and rubbed it across the prisoner's face. The ugly scar which ran from eye to chin, twisting his upper lip horribly, peeled off like bark from a tree.

"Let me introduce you," cried Holmes, "to Mr. St. Clair."

"So be it," said St. Clair. "I have committed no crime, but I'd rather die than have my children ashamed of their father."

The inspector said that his secret would be safe, but that his beggary, which was against the law, must cease.

"I was an actor, then a reporter," said St. Clair. "To do an article on begging, I disguised myself with this scar and red wig, and affected a limp. I was amazed at the money I earned; I paid the fines gladly. I rented the room above the den to change my clothes, and devoted all my time to begging. When I married, my dear wife knew only that I had business in the City; on Monday she surprised me at the window. You know the rest; the den's manager mailed my note. To my relief, instead of being identified, I was arrested as my own murderer. Never will I beg again!"

A	M	O	K			I	G	O	R		A	T	O	M
S	A	F	E		S	N	A	K	E		R	I	V	E
C	L	I	P		C	A	M	E	B	A	C	K	A	T
H	A	T	T	E	R		S	H	E	R		E	L	A
		I	R	I	S		S	L	A	B				
	A	G	N	O	M	E	N		S	C	R	A	W	L
S	K	R		S	P	R	A	Y		K	A	T	H	E
L	I	O	N		S	T	R	E	W		T	H	I	N
I	T	W	A	S		S	E	T	H	S		O	C	T
D	E	S	O	T	O		S	W	I	N	I	S	H	
		S	I	F	T		E	S	E	S				
U	H	S		F	L	A	G		T	E	R	M	E	D
B	E	N	E	F	I	C	I	A	L		A	E	R	O
E	R	I	N		F	O	R	C	E		E	N	O	W
R	O	P	E		E	S	T	E		L	O	O	N	

While still at the village inn, Watson had remarked to Holmes, "You have evidently seen more in those rooms than I have."

"No, but I deduced more. You saw the dummy bell-rope, the tiny ventilator, Julia's bed clamped to the floor, keeping it in the same relative position to ventilator and rope. Clearly, the rope is a bridge for something passing through the hole down to the bed—all this in a room whose occupant has died mysteriously.

"In Roylott's room, you saw the small saucer of milk, scant ration for a cheetah. I deduced a small creature; the whipcord loop suggested a snake, possibly housed in the safe—which would account for the clanging noise. If this is so, then Roylott has trained a snake to return from Julia's room at his whistle."

Hours later, the two men kept their dark vigil in Julia's room. Suddenly, a quiet hissing sounded. Holmes struck a match, and lashed out at the rope with his cane. A low whistle was heard; the snake slithered back up the rope; a horrible cry swelled up.

"It's all over!" cried Holmes, dashing into Roylott's room. Round the dead man's brow was a yellow snake, with brown speckles. "It's the swamp adder, Watson! India's deadliest snake, whose poison is not detectable. Caned, in snakish anger it bit Roylott."

A	G	T	S		A	T	T	H	E		F	A	K	E
F	L	A	T		T	R	A	I	L		O	B	O	E
T	U	N	A		H	O	R	S	E		R	U	H	R
	E	S	T	H	E	T	E		M	E	E	T	L	Y
		I	O	N	A		P	E	N	S				
A	C	T	O	R	S		D	E	N	O	T	I	N	G
L	E	A	N	S		T	R	O	T	S		S	O	O
L	L	M		C	O	I	N	S			F	O	R	
O	L	E		P	O	K	E	Y		T	W	A	N	G
Y	O	D	E	L	L	E	D		C	O	A	R	S	E
	L	E	O	N		F	R	E	I					
D	E	M	E	A	N		F	R	O	S	T	E	D	
A	L	E	C		E	L	L	E	N		I	D	E	A
C	A	N	T		L	E	A	S	E		N	E	L	L
E	N	D	S		S	I	K	H	S		G	N	A	T

"But we can't *all* be wrong," cried the inspector, laughing. "What about Hatherley's twelve-mile drive to Stark's house?"

"Six out, six back," said Holmes. "When Hatherley got into Stark's carriage, the horse was fresh—hadn't trotted any miles."

"And what are they using the press for?" asked Watson.

"Ah, you remember the metallic deposit on the floor. Stark tried to kill our friend when he discovered it. The press is secretly producing a base metal alloy—for an illicit purpose."

"They are counterfeiters," said Bradstreet, "coining half-crowns by the thousand. We traced them to Reading, near Eyford, then lost the track. I think now we have got them."

Bradstreet was to be disappointed. As the train rolled into Eyford, they saw a huge column of smoke rising behind a clump of trees. The stationmaster said that the blaze the firemen were fighting had started in the night; the house's occupants had fled in a cart. Holmes and his companions hurried to the house.

"That's it," cried Hatherley, "the garden into which I fell!"

"The lamp which was crushed in the press," said Holmes, "set fire to the walls. And see these footsteps—broad ones and small ones—Ferguson and the young lady carried you to safety!"

```
B S A S █ A B B E █ █ F L I M
A T T U █ L E A S H █ R A N I
L A R D █ B A N T U █ A I R S
S M I D G E N S █ S E C R E T
A P P E A R S █ A B R A █ █ █
█ █ █ N E T █ P R A I S I N G
S T A L L █ M A I N E █ T O O
P I T Y █ D O L E D █ P E S O
U N O █ T O W E L █ E R R E D
R E P O R T E D █ A M E █ █ █
█ █ █ B E E R █ D R I V E A T
K I L L E D █ M A R R I A G E
I D E A █ O R A L E █ O R A N
S L A T █ N O T E S █ U N I S
S E R E █ █ C A S T █ S A N E
```

When Holmes returned, he found an astonished Watson viewing the epicurean supper for five that Holmes had ordered sent up.

The first to arrive was Lord St. Simon. "Your messenger," said he, bitterly, "gave me your note. Hatty's humiliated me!"

"There is no humiliation in pure accident," said Holmes.

Next came lovely Hatty and an alert, wiry, sunburnt man, introduced to St. Simon by Holmes as Mr. and Mrs. Francis Hay Moulton.

"Don't be angry, Robert," pleaded Hatty. "I should have told you when I saw Frank in the pew, and he passed me the note—but I was so rattled. You see, my first duty was to Frank. We were engaged; then Pa struck it rich and made us break up, but we married secretly, just before Frank left to prove he could make his fortune, too. Then I read Frank was killed when Indians attacked his mining camp. But he was alive, and traced me to London, but couldn't find me 'til he read about the church wedding. Then he followed me home, and signaled from the Park, and I just went to him. Some woman came talking about you, Robert—seems you had a secret, too. Mr. Holmes found us at the hotel. I wanted to disappear, but he said, like Frank, it wouldn't be right."

"Sorry I can't stay for supper," said St. Simon, stalking out.

Puzzle VIII: *The Adventure of the Beryl Coronet*

A	M	E	B	A	■	O	A	F	S	■	H	I	S	T
L	E	M	U	R	■	F	L	E	W	■	I	T	T	O
D	E	I	S	T	■	F	I	N	A	N	C	I	A	L
A	R	T	H	U	R	■	A	C	R	E	■	S	R	I
■	E	R	O	S	■	E	M	A	N	A	T	E	■	■
S	E	L	L	O	U	T	S	■	S	R	O	■	■	■
O	D	E	■	N	E	L	L	■	S	T	O	R	M	■
L	I	A	R	■	D	R	I	E	R	■	A	S	I	A
D	E	N	I	M	■	E	N	T	E	■	A	A	R	■
■	■	D	I	M	■	G	I	N	G	E	R	L	Y	■
A	T	S	I	X	E	S	■	T	I	E	N	■	■	■
S	H	E	■	U	L	U	A	■	G	O	D	O	W	N
G	R	A	P	P	L	I	N	G	■	R	U	B	I	N
O	E	I	L	■	O	T	O	E	■	G	E	S	T	E
D	E	N	Y	■	W	E	N	T	■	E	S	T	H	S

"I must tell you, Mr. Holder," said Holmes, "that Sir George and Mary have fled together. He is a villain—Mary knew nothing of such men; he won her easily. Last night, through the hall window, she told him of the coronet. He bent her to his will.

"I surmised, and Arthur has since acknowledged, that in the night your lad heard footsteps, rose, and saw Mary entering your dressing-room. Petrified, he watched as she came out with the coronet, went downstairs, and handed it out the window. He would not expose the woman he loved, but when she returned to her room he rushed outside. He struggled with Sir George for the coronet. Not until you accused him in your dressing-room did he realize that he had left a corner of it in the villain's hands.

"The story was written in the snow. Lucy had trysted with her one-legged man near the garden; Arthur had struggled with a booted man near the stables. Who was Boots, who gave him the coronet? Arthur had no reason to shield a servant, but he loved Mary. You had few visitors; among them only Sir George called often. I confirmed my suspicion by buying a pair of his boots. Then I confronted him at his home. When I promised no prosecution, he named the receiver to whom he had sold the gems."

Puzzle IX: *Silver Blaze*

```
J O H N ▮ C R I M P ▮ S A I L
A L O E ▮ L I N E R ▮ I N G A
W A S G O I N G T O ▮ L O O M
S M E A R E D ▮ E L E V A T E
▮ T I N ▮ ▮ R I L E ▮ ▮ ▮
B A R E N T S ▮ ▮ F I R S T S
L E E R ▮ P A R I S ▮ L O A
A S A S ▮ R E L I C ▮ A I G U
Z I G ▮ A E D E S ▮ N E E R
E R E C T S ▮ E S P A R T O
▮ A L A I ▮ ▮ C U T ▮ ▮
B E T T I N G ▮ A U R O R A L
E R I C ▮ D O U B L E L I F E
R I C H ▮ E T H E L ▮ I B I D
I S S Y ▮ D O S E S ▮ A S T A
```

"Yes, Colonel, Silver Blaze, in self-defense, killed Straker. My first clue was the curry. It was too monstrous a coincidence that Simpson should have come along with powdered opium on just the night a curry was being served; only Straker could have chosen the supper that night. Then, the stable dog's silence indicated that he knew the midnight visitor. The knife in Straker's hand was strange as a weapon, but not as an operating tool. It could be used to make a subcutaneous nick on a horse's tendons leaving no trace, but slightly laming the horse. Clearly, Straker had practiced on the sheep. He took Silver Blaze far from the stable, since the horse would have aroused the sleeping lads when he was cut. Straker picked up the cravat Simpson lost, possibly to secure the horse's leg. He got behind Blaze and struck a match, but the sudden glare and an animal's instincts made the horse lash out—his steel shoe struck Straker on the forehead.

"What drove Straker to lame Blaze so that he could win a great sum betting against him? The Bond Street bill gave me the answer. Men do not carry other people's bills in their pockets—Straker had led a double life. I proved this by taking his photograph to Bond Street, where he was identified as William Derbyshire."

```
  P L A C E     I N H I S
W R I T I N G   G O I N T O
R E G A T T A   N O D D E R S
A V A   S O M E O N E   E A N
T U T S   M I T R E     R T E
H E E L S   N A E   T O H O E
    A C H E S   T A P E R S
  B O Y A R S   B A K E R Y
T O P E R S   W R I E R
O V E R S   T A O   N A B O B
S I R   L O A T H   S E R O
E N E   M A R C H E R   P A N
T E T H E R S   E M E R A L D
  S T I N G O   R E T A I L S
  A S S E S   N E E D Y
```

"The newspaper!" yelled Holmes. "Listen: 'Murder and Attempted Robbery at Mawson's. Slayer Taken.' Here, Watson, read it aloud."

Watson read:

> An attempt at robbery that ended in a man's death and the criminal's capture occurred this afternoon at Mawson's, the financial house, which uses the latest safes and employs an armed watchman day and night. Last week a new clerk named Hall Pycroft was engaged; he was none other than Beddington, notorious forger-cracksman, who was thus able to obtain moldings of the locks.
>
> Mawson's clerks leave at midday on Saturday. Sergeant Tuson noticed a man with a carpetbag leaving at twenty past one. With the aid of Constable Pollock, he arrested him. The bag contained one hundred thousand pounds of American railway bonds. The watchman, his skull crushed, was found in a large safe. Inquiries are being made about Beddington's brother, who usually works with him.

"Human nature is a strange mixture, Watson," said Holmes. "Even a murderer can inspire his brother to suicide in grief over him."

Puzzle XI: *The Reigate Puzzle*

```
M O L T ■ D U M A ■ T O K A Y
A M I A ■ A L E C ■ O L L I E
T A B L A T U R E ■ E D E M A
C H E L S E A ■ E N M E S H
H A L O S ■ B I N D A ■
■ W R I T I N G ■ N A P S
I K E S ■ N O T A R ■ S O L O
D I D ■ A D O B A ■ N O T
E W E R ■ S I N A I ■ T E D S
M I N E ■ N E E D L E R ■
■ S W I S S ■ R A D I I
R E P O R T ■ M A I M E R S
A D O R E ■ B L A C K M A I L
F A C T S ■ E A S T ■ E N D E
F R O S T ■ N O T E ■ L E S T
```

An hour later, in Colonel Hayter's home, Holmes was discussing the case with Watson, the colonel, and elderly Mr. Acton.

"The key to the matter," said Holmes, "was the scrap of paper in the dead man's hand. If the 'burglar' had not torn the note from him, then Mr. Alec was the guilty one. It occurred to me, Mr. Acton, that the Cunninghams were the 'burglars' who had broken into your house, looking for a paper supporting your claim."

"Ah," said Acton, "but it was in my solicitors' strong box."

"It was important to find the rest of the note. Forrester was about to tell them, so I fell into my 'fit.' I got old Cunningham to write the word 'twelve' for comparison with the fragment; I was then sure I was on the right track. I had noticed Mr. Alec's dressing-gown when we examined the rooms. I caused a diversion by knocking down the oranges, and had just found the paper in the gown's pocket, when they were upon me. Their desperation confirmed their guilt. Old Cunningham told me that William had secretly followed them when they raided Mr. Acton's, and was blackmailing them. The note decoyed him to the house. William was interested in a lady named Annie; the note promised surprising information that would be of service to him and to her."

Puzzle XII: *The Crooked Man*

```
A S H E S █ L I S P █ K A L B
F L E S H █ O N E R █ I L I A
T A H O E █ R E C E S S I O N
R I A █ A W E S █ F U M I N G
A N D I R O N █ S A M E █ █
█ G E N █ I N B A T T L E
A L B E R T █ D I S C █ H E R
H O O T █ R E P █ K I N G
A D M █ A S E A █ P R E S T O
B I B L I C A L █ L E R █
█ A D A M █ H U S B A N D
B A S S E T █ T E S T █ V A E
B A T H S H E B A █ A B O V E
A R O E █ E G A D █ T O W E D
S E W S █ D O R Y █ E A S E S
```

"The case had many features of interest," said Holmes, "not the least of which was the statement Miss Jane Stewart made of hearing her mistress utter the word 'David.' I confess I did not grasp its significance at the time."

"It's the one thing I don't understand," said Watson. "If the husband's name was James, and the other was Henry, what was this talk about David?"

"That one word, my dear Watson, should have told me the whole story had I been the ideal reasoner which you are so fond of depicting. It was evidently a term of reproach."

"Of reproach?"

"Yes; Sergeant James Barclay had acted in much the same way as David. You remember the small affair of the soldier Uriah and his beautiful wife, Bathsheba? When David desired to marry her, he had Uriah placed in the forefront of the battle, so that he might be killed. My Biblical knowledge is a trifle rusty, but I believe that you will find the story in the first or second of Samuel."

Puzzle XIII: *The Naval Treaty*

```
K N E W   ▉   I T E M S   ▉   B E E N
N O V A   ▉   N O R M A   ▉   O M R I
A N E T   ▉   T A L E R   ▉   B E L L
P O R T E R S   ▉   G A S S E S
▉   L O U T   ▉   W E L L   ▉
A P P E N D   ▉   M I S L E A D S
M E A   ▉   S E D A N   ▉   A D L A I
A R T   ▉   R U N I C   ▉   O B L
S C O W L   ▉   D O N O R   ▉   N E O
S Y N O P S E S   ▉   N E R E I S
▉   U N E S   ▉   A G N I   ▉
A F A L S E   ▉   F R O N T A L
R A N D   ▉   S H A R E   ▉   G I V E
C R I B   ▉   T A N I S   ▉   O L A F
H O L E   ▉   O D E T S   ▉   F E L T
```

"I am dying to know how you got the treaty," said Phelps.

"I stayed in the village until dark," said Holmes, "then I set out for Briar-brae, where I hid behind the rhododendrons opposite your window. The blind was not down, and I could see Miss Harrison reading at the table. At ten o'clock she closed the shutters. Without her help, you would not have the treaty.

"About two o'clock the servants' door opened, and out stepped Mr. Harrison. He used a long-bladed knife to open your window. I had a perfect view of the inside of the room. He lit the candles on the mantelpiece, turned back a corner of the carpet, picked up a piece of board, drew out the papers, blew out the candles, and walked out the window. I was there, ready for him.

"Master Joseph flew at me with his knife, but I got the upper hand and the papers. He told me he had lost heavily dabbling in stocks. I let him go, but I wired particulars to Forbes this morning. If he catches him, good. If not, so much the better. I fancy your uncle would rather the affair never got to court."

"Why did he try the window on the first occasion," asked Watson, "when he might have entered by the door?"

"Ah," said Holmes, "he would have had to pass seven bedrooms."

Puzzle XIV: *The Adventure of the Empty House*

Seated again in his favorite chair near the fire, with his friend Watson opposite him, Holmes spoke of his brush with Moran.

"After Moriarty's death, the police captured several members of his gang, but Moran was too clever to be incriminated. I knew of the existence of the air-gun. So long as Moran was free in London, my life would hardly have been worth living. But with the murder of Ronald Adair, I knew my chance had come. When I was seen by his sentinel, he could not fail to connect my sudden return with his crime, and be terribly alarmed. I was sure he would try to get me out of the way *at once*, and would bring the air-gun for that purpose. I left him an excellent mark in the window, and alerted the police.

"I have long been aware that Moran played foul at cards. On the day he was killed, Adair must have discovered this, and probably spoke to Moran privately. It is unlikely that a youngster like Adair would at once have made a hideous scandal. Figuring out the money he should return, Adair had locked his door so that his mother might not surprise him at his task."

	P	A	L	P		I	B	O	S		F	R	O	M
M	A	N	I	A		N	E	W	T		I	O	L	E
A	N	T	I	C		N	A	N	A		N	A	P	A
B	E	I		K	R	A	S		R	E	G	R	E	T
		S	L	E	E	T		U	R	G	E			
F	L	E	E	T	N	E	S	S		G	R	I	E	F
L	I	P	A	S	E		T	E	C	S		M	M	E
E	S	S		G	N	A	R	L			P	E	T	
A	L	I		S	E	A	L		A	S	P	R	E	E
M	E	S	N	E		R	E	M	I	T	T	E	R	S
		O	R	A	D		A	M	A	S	S			
T	E	N	N	E	R		A	S	S	N		S	E	C
O	M	O	O		A	W	N	S		D	A	I	N	O
O	M	I	T		R	A	T	E		B	L	O	O	D
K	A	L	E		A	X	E	S		Y	E	N	S	

After his men had led Oldacre away, Lestrade turned to Holmes. "You have saved McFarlane, and my career. How can I thank you?"

"Just change your report, Lestrade. Do not mention me; the work is its own reward. Now, let us see where the rat lurked."

A lath-and-plaster partition had been run across the corridor six feet from the end, with a door cunningly concealed in it. A few articles of furniture, food, and documents were within.

"In examining the house after you showed me the thumbprint, I found the top corridor six feet shorter than the one below; it was clear where he was. His housekeeper was his confederate. As to the thumbprint: By plan or by chance Oldacre got McFarlane to secure one of the packet seals by putting his thumb on it. No doubt you will find it among the documents he took into his retreat."

"What was the object of Oldacre's deception?" asked Lestrade.

"To wreak vengeance against Mrs. McFarlane, and, as he had lost monies in secret speculations, to swindle his creditors by disappearing and starting life again elsewhere under a new name. He has paid large checks to a Mr. Cornelius, none other than himself. It was a masterful plan, ruined by its creator. When you tell of it, Watson, make the charred remains and blood those of a rabbit."

```
Y A M . . A B A S . . O B O E
A R I A . P A S T A . F R O M
H A R P O O N E R S . F I N I
. P E T E R S . O P T I M A L
. . I S T . U N I O N . .
C O M T E . A N G R Y . S C I
E S A U . I C I . A S H C A N
A C I D . N I C E R . E R S T
S A M E D I . O N E . W I T H
E R S . I T E R S . L A P S E
. . B R I A N . C O S .
S T I L L A S . S I G N E D
L A N A . L I T T L E O N E S
E P I C . S E R A I . T I M E
W E A K . R A G A . D I A
```

"Have you ever tried to drive a harpoon through a body, Hopkins?" asked Holmes, as they breakfasted next morning. "No? Tut, tut, you must pay attention to details. Was Neligan's profile on Carey's blind? No. I hear footsteps, Watson, so have your revolver handy—ah, Mrs. Hudson, show the men in one by one."

The first two men were quickly dismissed, but the third, Patrick Cairns, a fierce, huge man, was hired as harpooner after Holmes had seen his papers. As he bent to sign on, Holmes snapped handcuffs on him, but it took Watson's revolver to subdue him.

"I did not murder Black Peter," said Cairns. "I *killed* him when he reached for his knife. I'll tell you all. I was harpooner on the *Sea Unicorn*. August '83 we picked up a craft in a gale and took on a man with a tin box. The next night I saw the skipper put him over the rail, and held my tongue until last week. First night I saw Carey he agreed to give me money, but two nights later he was drunk, violent—we quarreled, I killed him, took the box, but forgot my pouch on the table. After I left I saw another man go into the hut, and leg it out fast! Don't know what *he* wanted. I was afraid to sell the shares in the box. Then I saw the advertisement for harpooners and high wages, and here I am."

I	T	E	M		S	G	T	S			G	P	O	S
N	E	A	T		T	O	Y	E	D		R	A	M	I
T	A	S	S		O	U	N	C	E		O	U	S	T
E	S	E		I	L	L	E		C	A	U	L	K	S
R	E	L	A	T	E	D		H	O	S	P			
		N	I	N		R	I	C	H		O	R	A	
B	U	S	T	S		S	I	L	T	Y		B	E	L
A	V	I	S		S	I	L	L	S		M	I	N	T
G	E	M		W	A	X	E	S		B	U	T	T	O
S	A	P		A	F	T	S		D	O	S			
		A	D	A	H		C	O	N	T	A	I	N	
M	U	R	D	E	R		D	A	Z	E		L	O	O
A	R	I	D		I	N	A	N	E		P	I	N	T
C	E	D	E		S	A	T	A	N		A	B	I	T
E	Y	E	R		P	A	L	S		R	I	C	O	

When Lestrade arrived at Baker Street the next evening, he reported that Beppo had refused to talk about the busts.

Mr. Sandeford, of Reading, was ushered in. The elderly man carried a carpetbag, from which he drew a bust of Napoleon.

"Thank you," said Holmes, "and here are your ten pounds."

As Sandeford left, Holmes shattered the bust with his hunting crop. He picked up a fragment with a dark object embedded in it.

"The black pearl of the Borgias!" he cried triumphantly. "I reasoned that Beppo had hidden a thing of great value in one of the busts, but had been unable to retrieve it because of his imprisonment. My newspaper files showed that the pearl was stolen from the Princess of Colonna a few days before Beppo's arrest. Her maid, Lucretia Venucci, was suspected, but never arrested. Beppo probably stole the pearl from Pietro, who was carrying the snapshot to trace him, not to identify him. Beppo had the pearl on him when the police were on their way to Gelder & Co. Six plaster casts were drying in the passage; he hid it in one of them. His cousin at Gelder's told him of the sales to Hudson and to Harding. He obtained work at Hudson's and located three of them; an employee of Harding's gave him the addresses of the other three."

S	P	A	S	■	S	M	A	L	L	■	B	I	T	T
H	E	T	H	■	P	O	N	E	S	■	E	T	A	H
O	A	R	S	■	I	N	A	I	D	■	L	A	K	E
E	R	I	■	S	K	A	T	■	■	R	I	L	E	Y
S	L	A	S	H	E	D	■	S	O	I	E	■		
■		L	O	S	■	F	E	L	L	F	R	O	M	
S	C	R	A	P	■	S	E	G	A	L	■	A	G	O
A	L	U	M	■	O	N	E	O	F	■	P	I	L	L
M	A	H	■	A	R	I	L	S	■	H	O	N	E	D
P	Y	R	A	M	I	D	S	■	B	U	M	■	■	
■		C	A	G	E	■	J	U	M	P	I	N	G	
W	I	T	C	H	■	B	E	T	E	■	D	O	E	
R	O	U	E	■	S	H	A	L	T	■	H	Y	D	E
I	N	A	N	■	T	A	B	L	E	■	I	L	U	S
T	E	N	T	■	S	T	A	Y	S	■	E	L	S	E

Gilchrist appeared dismayed to find Bannister in the room.

"We want to know, Mr. Gilchrist," said Holmes, "how a man like you came to commit such an action as that of yesterday."

Gilchrist cast a look of horror and reproach at Bannister.

"No, no, sir," cried Bannister, "I never said one word!"

"But now you have," said Holmes. "Be frank, Mr. Gilchrist."

Gilchrist buried his face in his hands, and burst into tears.

"Come, come," said Holmes kindly. "I shall speak for you."

Holmes related how Gilchrist, carrying his jumping shoes, had seen the papers through the window, the key in the door, and was copying a page when he suddenly heard Soames at the door; how he had snatched his shoes (which dropped a pellet and cut the table), and had hidden in the bedroom until Soames had left; how Bannister had sat on telltale evidence.

"This morning I got a bit of the black clay from the jumping pit," said Holmes. "And Bannister had sat on—? Ah, gloves."

"Have you nothing to say, Gilchrist?" cried Soames.

"Yes, sir. Here is a letter I wrote to you last night. Bannister made me see that I should not profit by cheating. I felt that I could not remain here. I leave today for a post in Rhodesia."

"Sir Jabez Gilchrist," said Bannister, "was my old master."

Puzzle XIX: *The Adventure of the Golden Pince-Nez*

```
T R O D   S T R I P ■ G R O G
A H M E   N O E N D ■ R U S E
B E I N   S L A T S ■ A N T A
S A T I N ■ E D E ■ E S T E R
■ ■ M U R D E R E S S ■ ■
A E T ■ R O O ■ N O T ■ O S S
G L A S S E S ■ E N H A N C E
A L I K E ■ ■ ■ E S T O P
M I N I M U M ■ W I T H O U T
A S E ■ A R I ■ A N I ■ P T A
■ ■ S I N S W H I C H ■ ■
C O U L D ■ S A I ■ S O A P S
H A V E ■ S T I N T ■ U R A L
O K A Y ■ M E T E R ■ S A N O
O Y L S ■ S P A S M ■ E D I T
```

"The case hinged on the pince-nez," said Holmes, as he and his companions traveled back to town. "It was clear that the wearer must be very blind without them. I set down as an impossibility her walking back along a narrow strip of grass without a false step, save in the unlikely case that she had a second pair of glasses. I had to consider seriously the hypothesis that she remained in the house. The similarity of the two corridors made clear that in her terrified flight she might take the one leading to the professor's room. I examined the room for a hiding place. The carpet seemed continuous and firmly nailed; I ruled out a trapdoor. But there might be a recess behind the bookcases. I noted that books were piled all over the floor, but that one bookcase was left clear. I dropped cigarette ashes in front of it. By upsetting the cigarette box, I obtained an excellent view of the floor, and saw that the lady had come out during our absence. I also knew that it was she who had made the scratch on the bureau, for the professor's key had no trace of varnish on it. Well, Hopkins, I congratulate you on a successful case. You are going to headquarters, no doubt. Watson and I will drive to the Russian Embassy."

```
S H A D   C U T U P   B A C K
T A C O   A S O R E   O T O E
E L E C   S C E N T   T E R N
P O R T I A   S I S T E R S
  O F B A D   T I O
C A R R I A G E   I A M B I C
O B I S   E A T O N   E L A
M A N   H U N T I N G   D O G
U S S   O N T H E   T O V E
S H E A R S   T R A N S F E R
  M A T   O S T I A
W H E E L O F   T E R A I S
H O W E   R A M I E   D I S H
O V E R   E R I C S   O L E O
S E R S   D E B I T   M E E T
```

Holmes had shot aniseed (a scent irresistible to draghounds, he told Watson) over a back wheel of Dr. Armstrong's brougham. Pompey, on a leash, led them from Cambridge to a country road, up and down lanes, back to Cambridge, and then on in the opposite direction.

"So this is how he gave me the slip!" exclaimed Holmes. "By Jove! here is his carriage coming back. Quick, Watson—quick!"

Hiding under a hedge, they caught a glimpse of the doctor, his head sunk on his hands. Pompey led them at last to a lonely cottage in a field, from which came a low sound of misery and despair. Suddenly, they heard the doctor's carriage returning.

"We must see what it all means before he comes," cried Holmes, opening the door. A woman, young and beautiful, was lying dead upon a bed; kneeling beside her was a young man racked with sobs.

"Mr. Godfrey Staunton?" asked Holmes gently. The man nodded.

When Dr. Armstrong entered, Holmes took him aside and promised that the facts would be kept out of the papers.

"I misjudged you," said the doctor. "His uncle would have disinherited Godfrey had he known he married his landlady's daughter—a fine young lady. It was her father who came to Godfrey's hotel."

```
E D E L █ B O U N D █ E D O M
L A D Y █ S U P E R █ N I P A
U N D E R S T A T E █ D E A R
L E A S H █ R T E S █ O N L Y
█ █ E V E R █ S I F █ █
K I L L E R █ E M Y S █ N O T
A S I A █ A S E A █ M A O R I
I N E R T I A █ S L E P T A N
L O B A R █ I S T O █ I B L E
S T E █ I T C H █ F R A Y E D
█ H O I █ E S T A █
W I R E █ R E A P █ T R A S H
A V O W █ A T T A C H E D T O
C A P E █ N E H R U █ N A O S
O N E R █ A S S E T █ T H A T
```

"I fell in love with Mary Fraser the moment I saw her on the ship," said Croker, "but on her side it was friendship. Then I heard she had married well—I was happy for her. I never thought to see her again, but my new boat was not ready, so I had to wait a month with my people in Sydenham. One day I met Theresa, her maid. She told me everything; it nearly drove me mad. The drunken hound, that he should dare to raise his hand to her! I wanted to see her before I left. We were standing in the dining-room, in all innocence, as God is my judge, when he rushed in and welted her across the face with his stick. I had sprung for the poker, and it was a fair fight. See here, on my arm, where his first blow fell. Mary's screams brought Theresa; it was her plot as much as mine. We must make it appear that burglars had done the thing. I needed a rope, and as I did not want the bell to ring, I swarmed up and cut it. I lashed Mary in her chair, and frayed out the end of the rope to make it look natural. I dropped the silver in the pond, and made off. And that's the whole truth. I thought the police never could have seen through our dodge."

"The police haven't," said Holmes, "nor will they. So long as the law does not find some other victim, your secret is safe."